BEYOND DIALOGUE

JOHN B. COBB, JR.

BEYOND DIALOGUE

Toward a Mutual Transformation of Christianity and Buddhism

FORTRESS PRESS, **Philadelphia**

Library of Congress Cataloging in Publication Data

Cobb, John B.
Beyond dialogue.
1. Mahayana Buddhism—Relations—Christianity.
2. Christianity and other religions—Mahayana Buddhism.
I. Title.
BQ7436.C57C63 1982 261.2'43 82-8389
ISBN 0-8006-1647-2

9596D82 Printed in the United States of America 1-1647

Contents

Preface

AN INESCAPABLE FEATURE of Christian self-understanding is the recognition that we share the world with people of other religious traditions. This was very apparent indeed during the first centuries of the Christian movement, and it has forced itself upon Christian attention again in the past two centuries.

The most common Christian response to this recognition has been to assume that those who are different from us are for that reason inferior. They lack the saving truth we possess and, accordingly, it is our task to convert them. Usually this has been by persuasion, but Christians have not always been above using more forceful methods.

In the twentieth century, and especially since World War II, Christian confidence in Christian superiority has eroded. Appreciative understanding of other traditions has become relatively widespread, and criticism of Christian arrogance and imperialism is commonplace. This is a great gain for faith. But it is accompanied by theological confusion.

The focus of this confusion is Christology. We have believed that there is no name under heaven by which people can be saved other than that of Jesus Christ. Because of that conviction we have done all we could to bring others to faith in him. Now we find that our achievements have been in many ways ambiguous. Does that mean that we were wrong in our belief in the universal and exclusive salvific power of Jesus Christ? If so, what is the theological meaning and reality of Jesus Christ? Should we abandon all efforts to proclaim him to those who do not now believe? Or should we distinguish between those who have satisfactory Ways of salvation through other saviors and those who are yet in need of such a Way? If so, how?

Unfortunately, there is now a widespread sense that our choice is either to continue our belief in Christian superiority and to act upon it or to see Jesus as one savior among others. The former choice turns Christ into an instrument of our arrogance. The latter abandons the universal meaning and truth of Christ so central to our historic faith. Is there no other option?

Certainly there must be. Neither the Roman Catholic church nor the World Council of Churches has accepted either horn of this dilemma. Both are working painfully toward a Christology which avoids both imperialism and relativism. This book is set in this context.

The commitment of the Roman Catholic church and the World Council of Churches is to both witness and dialogue. Just how these are to be related remains puzzling. Witness assumes that one has a truth worth sharing. Dialogue assumes that the partner is worth listening to as well as addressing. There is no contradiction, but there are tensions.

This book is entitled *Beyond Dialogue*. The title is not intended to disparage dialogue. It is only through dialogue that we can go beyond dialogue. But dialogue that does not intend to go beyond itself stagnates. Through dialogue people come to understand one another better and learn to cooperate better. In dialogue they may even learn from one another ideas and insights that will enrich their several Ways. But when the Christian witnesses to Christ in the dialogue, the hope must be to do more than provide minor insights. Christ is understood only when Christ becomes the center around which life is lived. Similarly, when an adherent of another Way speaks to us of what is decisive for that Way, the intention is to tell us of something utterly indispensable to full human life.

It is often stressed that the purpose of dialogue is not to convert. People of other religious Ways will not enter the dialogue if its purpose, from the Christian side, is to convert them to Christianity. One continuing problem with establishing dialogue is that so many are suspicious that for Christians this is another instrument of conversion. Therefore dialogue must limit itself to an exchange that is not intended to fulfill its own deeper intentions! Precisely for that reason we must go beyond dialogue. If we are serious about Jesus Christ, we must intend that others learn the truth of Christ. But this does not mean that we can fall back from dialogue to a witness that has not passed through dialogue. Instead we must pass through a dialogue in which we truly hear the truth that the other has to teach us.

To hear in an authentic way the truth which the other has to teach us is to be transformed by that truth. Once we have heard the truth of Islam, our Christian witness cannot remain what it was. And in our day only those Christians who have really heard that truth can deserve a serious hearing from Muslims. Further, only those Christians who have been transformed by appropriation of the universal truth found in other religious Ways can proclaim the universal truth of Jesus Christ without a false imperialism. It will be in the process of multiple transformations through and beyond multiple dialogue that the Christian movement as a whole will gain an adequate understanding of the universal truth of Jesus Christ on a new and more faithful level.

A very special case is the dialogue with Judaism. Christianity is a child of Judaism, and it would be an understatement to say that we have treated our parent badly. Too often we have assumed that from the beginning we have already included all that Judaism offers to us. We have, accordingly, ignored the truth and reality of the living religious movement in our midst. Until we have learned to speak of Jesus Christ with deep appreciation for the truth and reality of living Judaism, we will contribute to the continuation of the ugliest of all Christian crimes—our crime against the Jews.

This pattern of learning from other movements is not new for Christians. In the first centuries of Christian history the church appropriated a great deal from Neoplatonism, which was its chief competitor in the Hellenistic world. If Christianity had not appropriated the truth of Neoplatonism, it is doubtful that it would have gained the wide acceptance which it in fact achieved.

In the modern world the greatest challenge to Christianity for the minds of Western people has been science and the modes of thinking which it has inspired. Insofar as the church in modern Europe has avoided being driven into a ghetto, this has been a result of its assimilation of, and transformation by, scientific wisdom. On the other hand, the church's resistance to appropriation of the universal truth offered by modern science has been a chief factor in the decline of conviction within its ranks and the weakening of its capacity to shape and guide modern thought.

Of course the church has suffered from uncritical assimilation of elements of Neoplatonism, and it has been right in rejecting some aspects of the world view usually associated with modern science. Nevertheless, the health of the church is highly correlated with its openness to receive the truth of other traditions with which it is in contact. We must earnestly hope that in the continuing encounter of Christians with participants in other religious Ways, Christians will be increasingly attentive to what non-Christians have to teach and will be ready to be changed through new insight.

Dialogue is not the appropriate relation to all alien movements. It is grounded in basic respect, in the recognition of wisdom and integrity. There are movements such as Nazism and the Ku Klux Klan in which Christians do not recognize the requisite wisdom and integrity. There are many movements about which we are uncertain. But the time is past when sensitive Christians can question the presence in our world of many alien movements which rightly claim our respect and from which we have something to learn. It is in relation to these that dialogue is appropriate.

Prior knowledge of the religious tradition from which the other speaks is beneficial to dialogue. But it is a mistake to demand too much here. If only those Christians who are scholars in the field of Islamics take part in dialogue with Muslims, the deeper purposes of dialogue are unlikely to be realized. Too often in this country the dialogue with representatives of other traditions has been in this way handed over to historians of religion, many of whom are not committed to the Christian faith and its fresh articulation. Dialogue with Buddhism is not primarily the province of Buddhologists but rather of Christian theologians who are, for the most part, but little informed about the Buddhist traditions.

The dialogue with Buddhists will, of course, have failed if Christian theologians who take part in it are not stimulated thereby to learn from the work of Buddhologists. They must understand enough to see that no dialogue partners can possibly speak for all the segments of Buddhism any more than any Christian theologian can speak for all branches of Christianity. But the purpose of dialogue, in distinction from scholarship, is to encounter living representatives of an alien religious Way—individuals who find that Way adequate and salvific but who are also involved in the continuing process of understanding it in an ever-changing situation. In an important sense the texts studied by the scholars remain static, whereas in a successful dialogue both partners are engaged in fresh thinking. The research into the traditions which the dialogue should stimulate will be for the sake of participating more effectively in the present engagement.

I have made this point partly to justify my own participation in this field. I am not a historian of religion, and I do not have a scholar's knowledge of any tradition with the partial exception of my own. My approach is that of a Christian theologian seeking to understand the Christian faith in a pluralistic context. I believe that through dialogue I have learned enough about some other traditions to understand something of the implication their wisdom has for my understanding of Christianity. It is this that I would share.

Christians cannot decide before dialogue what they will learn from it. Each dialogue will be different, and there is an indefinite number of potential dialogue partners from each of whom something of importance to us can and should be learned. No one Christian can engage in all of these dialogues. The selection of dialogue will always have about it an element of the arbitrary.

My own limited dialogue has been with Mahayana Buddhists, especially Zen and Pure Land Buddhists in Japan. Hence this book will be an exploration of what it can mean for Christians to go beyond dialogue in relation to these particular religious Ways. The results of going through and beyond dialogue with Jews, Muslims, Hindus, Marxists, or adherents of the primal vision of Africa have been and will be diverse. The correlation of the results of such adventures is a task for the future.

This book is about the church's mission in relation to other religious Ways and their serious adherents. In this connection it argues against proselytism as a goal. But it would be unfortunate if this argument should be taken as encouraging the present failure of progressive Christians even to attempt to win to the church those millions in our own society and in others around the world who are cut off from the wisdom of any of the world's great religious traditions and who participate in no communities of serious purpose.

These millions are to be found in Japan as well as in the United States. Many of them there are nominally Buddhist as many of them here are nominally Christian. Most of them both there and here embody these traditions only in superstitious and idolatrous forms. When Buddhists succeed in converting such "Christians" to Buddhism, we should rejoice in the name of Christ. If Christians can draw into the Christian community in Japan nominal Buddhists of this sort, we should rejoice in the name of Christ. We should not use the fact that dialogue is now in fashion to reduce our efforts to incorporate into the church those who need its saving word and life. But evangelism of this sort is not the subject of this book.

Chapter One surveys the history of Christian teaching with respect to followers of other religious Ways. It shows how the dialogical mode has come into prominence in recent times.

Chapter Two summarizes recent theological discussion of the meaning of our pluralistic situation for Christian theology and then proceeds to critical evaluation and constructive theological statement. It points to the need to deal concretely with particular dialogue partners. The remainder of the book focuses on Mahayana Buddhism.

Chapter Three surveys the history of Western efforts to understand the key Buddhist notion of Nirvana, distinguishing the scholarly, the philosophical, and the experiential or religious approaches.

Chapter Four offers my own understanding of Nirvana as this has been formed in dialogue. It is presented in its sharp contrast to received modes of Christian thinking.

Chapter Five returns to constructive theology, attempting to appropriate Buddhist wisdom in a transformed Christianity.

Chapter Six proposes that a Christianity transformed by its encounter with Buddhism can offer Jesus Christ to Buddhism in a realistic and helpful way.

Although explicit discussion of Alfred North Whitehead in this book is quite limited, his conceptuality plays a large role in guiding the appropriation of Buddhist truth. A brief postscript is directed to those who question my employment of this philosophy in the service of going beyond dialogue.

Much of the work that lies behind these chapters was done during a six-month stay in Washington, D.C. in 1976 as a fellow of the Woodrow Wilson International Center for Scholars. I wrote three lectures during that period which I gave as the Armstrong Lectures at Kalamazoo College in that year. Much of the material can be found in this book, especially in Chapters Three, Four, and Five.

A six-month stay in Japan in 1978 made possible by an invitation from Rikkyo University enabled me to pursue my interest in the relation between Christianity and Mahayana Buddhism. Much of what is now Chapter Six was written at that time. Under the titles "Can a Christian be a Buddhist, Too?" and "Can a Buddhist be a Christian, Too?", *Japanese Religions* published much of the material in Chapters Five and Six. Chapters Three through Six correspond closely to the Rall Lectures for 1979 at Garrett-Evangelical Theological Seminary. I delivered these under the title "Nirvana and the Christian Faith." The invitation to give the Earl Lectures at the Pacific School of Religion in 1981 offered me a chance to summarize the argument for the entire book in a quite abridged form.

For the understanding of Buddhism which is expressed in the book I am particularly indebted to dialogues with Professor Ryusei Takeda of Ryukoku University and Professor Masao Abe, recently retired from Nara University and now teaching at the Claremont Graduate School. Others from whose suggestions and critical responses I have benefited include Jay McDaniel, Francis Cook, and Donald Swearer. I have been assisted in the preparation of the manuscript for publication by Jan Ritzau, Robert Flaherty, and the always helpful secretarial staff at the School of Theology at Claremont. I am genuinely grateful to all, and especially to Madeline McReynolds. I am particularly indebted to Teresa Shaw for preparing the index.

BEYOND DIALOGUE

CHAPTER ONE

The Road to Dialogue

MUCH IN THE CONTEMPORARY SITUATION is new. Christians are appreciatively aware of other religious traditions or Ways, and the significance of these Ways for Christian self-understanding has become a central theological concern. Whereas, prior to the nineteenth century, thematic consideration of other Ways and their meaning for Christian theology was rare, today it is inescapable.

Nevertheless, Christians have been responding to other Ways throughout history. Our responses have been diverse and differentiated. As appropriate response becomes more and more decisive for us, we cannot simply turn to the past to learn what that is. Indeed, when we review the past with eyes that are opened to the greatness and goodness of other Ways, we are driven to repentance for our arrogance. Precisely where Christian teaching about other Ways has been most fully developed, as in relation to Judaism, we have the greatest need for repentance. But if we are to repent wisely and well, that is, if we are to turn into a new and more appropriate course, we cannot simply ignore our past. We must understand it and build upon it as well as criticize it.

This chapter offers a survey of the Christian struggle to understand Christian faith in relation to other Ways. It is divided into two sections. The first is a brief sketch of the first nineteen centuries. The second is a somewhat more detailed treatment of recent developments, especially of the widespread acceptance of a dialogical relation to other Ways. Attention is directed to the World Council of Churches and the Roman Catholic church, but theories of some individual Christian thinkers closely related to that discussion are also considered.

I. Christian Teaching Into the Twentieth Century

The most important source of Christian self-understanding, by far, is the Bible. Hence, the relation of Israel and early Christianity to other religious communities and the biblical understanding of other religious traditions are of utmost relevance for us. But thus far students of the Bible have not dealt with this question extensively. A few general comments on biblical views can be offered in hopes that before long Old and New Testament scholars will provide us with more light. The traditions which developed into our canon are marked by massive assimilation of material from the religious traditions of Canaan, Egypt, Babylonia, Persia, and Greece. Nevertheless, the dominant element in the consciousness of the biblical writers was the contrast and opposition of the faith of Israel to the religious practices and beliefs of the Gentiles. This duality characterizes both the Old and the New Testaments.

The sense of contrast and opposition was not illusory. Israel had its own way of life which became more and more distinctive as time went by. Israel's adoption of materials from other cultures also involved their transformation. Although the Jewish community was often threatened by assimilation to dominant cultures, there was always sufficient continuing resistance to prevent the loss of its distinctive place and role.

Those Jews who believed that in Jesus the promises of God were fulfilled were equally clear that they had a distinctive message of supreme importance. They could borrow freely from Gentile culture without any threat to their own identity. The identity of these Jewish believers in Jesus remained, through much of the first century, Jewish. They struggled to clarify the true and appropriate form of that identity in the light of the cross and resurrection of Jesus. This could involve a harsh polemic against those Jews who refused to accept Jesus as the Messiah. It did not involve viewing Judaism as a religion over against Christianity. In Romans 9–11 Paul shows that it entailed the view that God has providentially delayed the acceptance by the Jews of their Messiah so that a space could be opened up for Gentiles.

For a brief period the fact that Christians understood themselves to be Jews led to a debate as to whether those Gentiles who became Christians should also accept the full Jewish law. The crucial issue was circumcision, a requirement that had deterred many Gentiles, attracted to Judaism independently of the Christian claim, from full union with the Jewish community. Paul was the key figure in the struggle to show that with the coming of the Christ the necessity of obedience to the law was ended. The true Israel was now the eschatological community of those who had faith in Christ and awaited the final consummation. Every person as an individual was invited to enter this community. Paul dealt subtly and profoundly with the differences between Jews and Gentiles, but he saw no need to discriminate thematically the relative merits of the alternative Gentile traditions.

Although Paul saw salvation as coming only through Jesus Christ, he did not simply dismiss as evil everything in the Gentile world. He appropriated many of its rhetorical forms and ethical teachings. He explicitly taught that conscience functioned among the Gentiles analogously to the way the law functioned among Jews. God was manifest to Gentiles as well as Jews in the "things that have been made" (Rom. 1:20). Paul attacked the idolatrous distortions that characterized Gentile culture, but his polemic placed him on the side of other Gentiles who shared this condemnation of idolatry. He certainly was not issuing a wholesale denunciation of every form of Gentile life and thought.

In Paul's view the pagan gods were not simply distorted forms of the true God or products of human imagination but real beings. He refers to them with contempt as "weak and beggarly elemental spirits" (Gal. 4:9). Through faith in Christ the Gentile could come to know rightly the true God who had been known already by the Jews.

Luke pictures Paul as preaching to Epicurean and Stoic philosophers in Athens (Acts 17:16–31). In the sermon here placed on Paul's lips, Paul quotes from pagan writers, acknowledging the truth of what they have said. He presents his message as the truth of a God whom, without knowledge, the audience already worshiped. In general Luke pictures Christianity as bringing enlightenment and as purifying existing beliefs and practices.

A consistent contrast between Christianity and paganism is

found in the distinction between faith on the one side and efforts to manipulate deity on the other. Faith orients us to the divine will and to trusting ourselves to that will. Pagan practices, as perceived in the New Testament, seek ways to gain from the gods what is wanted by human beings without regard to the divine will. For example, Jesus is quoted as follows: "And in praying do not heap up empty phrases as the Gentiles do; for they think that they will be heard for their many words" (Matt. 6:7).

John's Gospel is the most Christocentric of all, and much of its language suggests a radically negative view of religious traditions other than Christianity, including Judaism (cf. John 8:42–44). Nevertheless, its prologue posits that the everlasting Word, or Logos, has always illumined everyone. This doctrine opened the way to a positive appreciation of persons and religious movements outside the Jewish and Christian orbits. On the other hand, John's Gospel presents the Jews as the antagonists of Jesus. The account of the crucifixion in John, as in the other Gospels, places the primary blame upon "the Jews." This gave rise over the centuries to the epithet "Christ-killer" applied indiscriminately to all Jews, undergirding much of the anti-Jewish teaching and action that have so deeply colored and corrupted the corporate life of Christian churches.

There is thus no one view of other religious traditions or Ways in the New Testament. The topic is never thematically discussed. Attention is directed instead to what Christ has done and can do for persons as persons. The distinction between Jew and Gentile is presupposed and occasionally discussed. The major point is that this distinction is overcome in Christ. There is an ongoing struggle to understand the failure of the Jewish people as a whole to accept Jesus as Messiah; there is a growing and successful mission to the Gentiles; and there are scattered indications of beliefs about the religious practices of Gentiles. Distinctions among Gentile traditions are made implicitly inasmuch as insights and ideas from some are freely borrowed, while idolatry is consistently condemned. But such distinctions are not reflectively considered. The scattered and diverse comments could be used in subsequent generations to support a wide variety of Christian positions.

By the second century Christianity had separated itself from Judaism in its self-understanding. Judaism now appeared to Christians as a separate community and religious tradition which must be declared to be in fundamental error for having misunderstood its own scriptures and denied its promised Messiah. The attitude toward Judaism was harshly polemical, paving the way for the Christian persecutions of Jews which have marked and marred so much of Christian history. This did not, of course, mean that Christians saw Jews as remote. On the contrary, they worshiped the same God and read the same scriptures. The fight was within the family, and all the more bitter for that reason. The anti-Jewish polemic was surpassed in violence only by that directed against the Gnostics and others regarded as Christian heretics.

During the second century the distinction between pagan religious practices and the religio-philosophical schools became more explicit. Justin Martyr viewed the gods of the pagans as demons, but as he confronted Greek philosophy he found much that he admired and adopted. This affinity he attributed to the work of the Logos. The Logos had enabled Greek writers to grasp many fragments of the truth, but only Christianity has the full truth because the Logos has come in its fullness in Christ. Thus while Christ stands against idolatry and the worship of demons, Christ is the fulfillment of the fragmentary truth that is present in the world of Gentile thought.

Clement of Alexandria elaborates this further by identifying Greek philosophy as having played in the Greek world the schoolmaster role which in the Jewish world had been played by the law. It is not, then, merely a fragmentary grasp of the truth but a necessary preparation for the gospel. Not only Socrates and Plato, but also thinkers of Persia, India, and Egypt witnessed to the Logos. According to Irenaeus, "There is but one and the same God who, from the beginning to the end and by various dispensations, comes to the rescue of mankind."[1] St. Augustine could follow this through to the conclusion: "From the beginning of the human race, whosoever believed in [Christ], and lived in a pious and just manner according to His precepts, was undoubtedly saved by Him. . . . The true religion, although formerly set forth and practiced under other names and with other symbolic rites than it now has . . . is one and the same in both periods."[2]

The doctrine of Christ as the Logos thus encouraged a positive view of the thought of pre-Christian peoples, including their religious thought. This positive view in turn encouraged the assimilation of much Greek philosophy by the leading thinkers of the church. In the influential writings of Origen many Christian teachings were interpreted in Neoplatonic categories. Christian and pagan Neoplatonists worked side by side in Alexandria, and their disagreements in doctrine were often muted.

To a large extent the conversion of the pagan intelligentsia to Christianity required the assimilation into Christianity of what this intelligentsia found most convincing in its classical heritage. This included its poetry and its science; Basil of Caesarea declared that in pagan literature Christians could find something that "keeps the soul alive."[3] Further, this assimilation especially involved its philosophy, which by the time of the church fathers was interpreted through its Neoplatonic development. Many who were willing to abandon the traditional temple worship of the ancient gods could not rid themselves of the insights they had come to through the philosophical tradition. Even those who joined the church sometimes interpreted those Christian doctrines which conflicted with these insights as fitting only for the common people. It seems that the victory of the church over paganism was in part due "to the rule that the Christians assimilate pagan ideas, while the pagans do not appropriate Christian ones."[4]

Other Christians were more concerned to maintain the distinctiveness of Christian thinking over against the dominant cultural traditions. Tertullian is the most notable example. His major concern was to preserve the purity of Christian living, and his ethical rigorism led him to join the Montanists and eventually to establish his own sect. This was associated with the polemic against Gnosticism and accommodationism in general. "What is there in common," he asked, "between Athens and Jerusalem? What between the Academy and the Church? . . . Away with all proposals for a 'Stoic,' a 'Platonic,' or a 'dialectical' Christianity."[5] Yet even Tertullian in fact accepted much of classical culture and was selective in his denunciation.

In the fourth century the conversion of Constantine and the establishment of Christianity by the state turned Christian attitudes toward other religious movements into public policies. The earlier request for tolerance of Christianity by the state did not lead to the adoption of tolerance as a Christian principle. On the contrary, Christian leaders pressed the state to take action against the opponents of Christianity. The Christian empire was considerably less tolerant toward the Jews than the pagan empire had been, and leading Christian preachers such as Ambrose pressed the emperors to adopt more repressive policies. The church also used the state to persecute those who were regarded as heretics.

In relation to paganism a threefold distinction had developed by the fourth century. There was Greek philosophy taught especially in Athens and Alexandria. There were temples for public worship of the Greco-Roman gods and others, such as Sol, imported from the East. And there was a large range of magical and occult practices. The Christian emperors responded to these three in highly differentiated ways. They adopted extremely severe measures against the third, decreeing death to the magicians. They tolerated for some time public ceremonies at the pagan temples—even, occasionally, participating. They supported the philosophical schools, insofar as philosophy was clearly distinguished from the magical arts. Unfortunately, philosophy in Athens had become deeply involved with the occult, and it was this that led to the suppression of the Athenian school, while the school of Alexandria continued to be supported and included Christians among its teachers.

In rural areas, paganism remained a competitor with Christianity for centuries, but as it lost its intellectual and cultural leadership, it ceased to be a major threat. It was replaced in this role by the rise of Islam. In the seventh and eighth centuries much of what had been Christendom was conquered by Muslims. For centuries Islam represented a level of intellectual and cultural life far superior to that of the Christian West and at least equal to that of Byzantium. Hence the religion toward which Christians now had to formulate their attitudes was one that they experienced as a profound threat. Christendom was besieged, and it responded with outrage against the religion of the attackers. The hostility was not reduced when Western Christians took the offensive against the "infidel" in the Crusades.

The Muslim world treated the Jews far better than did Christians, who explicitly taught that although Jews must be allowed to survive, they should be kept in a condition of misery. Jews flourished in Muslim Spain and cooperated with the Muslims in building a great civilization. This close association of Jew and Muslim led to even worse treatment of the Jews by Christians. The term "infidel" which was the Christian battle cry against the Muslims was applied to Jews as well. The energies mustered to recover the Holy Land from the Muslims were directed frequently to the slaughter of defenseless Jews within Western Europe and along the Crusaders' routes. When the Muslims were driven out of Spain, Jews were given the choice of exile or conversion to Christianity. Those who accepted conversion but continued to practice elements of their own heritage were mercilessly punished by the inquisitors. Throughout Europe Jews who did not accept baptism were restricted and persecuted under church law in ever more vicious ways.

The Crusades were not the only Christian response to Islam. The advanced culture of Spain attracted the interest of Christian scholars, and through Muslim philosophers, especially Averroës, new interest and understanding of Aristotle stimulated Christian learning. St. Thomas Aquinas was in this way deeply indebted to Islam. His recognition of the presence of rational theology in Islam influenced the development of his conception of the power of reason to attain much knowledge of God. However, he emphasized that the Christian revelation is also required.

More radical spirits detached themselves from commitment to the specifics of Christian doctrine and found more promise in a friendly relation to Jews and Muslims. The court of Frederick II in Sicily was a haven for tolerance and skepticism. Of course, Christendom in general was shocked.

More important was the missionary response. This was particularly promoted by Ramon Lull (c.1233–c.1315). Christian missions were premised on the assumption that Islam was in error, but Lull did recognize the importance of understanding Islam, and as he studied it he found much to admire. He presented its teaching fairly and noted the fervor of its followers in comparison with the lukewarm faith of so many Christians.

Whereas Lull and the Christian missionaries sought the conversion of Muslims to Christianity, Nicholas of Cusa sought for peace between Christians, Jews, and Muslims through unity. At the time of the fall of Constantinople, 1453, he published *De Pace Fidei.*[6] He held that since all worshiped the same God, and since cultural differences in teaching and in forms of worship are acceptable, the three religions should unite. Although his terms of unification in fact involved the acceptance of some basic Christian teachings and practices, the book is remarkable for its irenic and tolerant tone. The acceptance of Christian teaching and practice does not require, in his view, joining the Christian church or acknowledging the authority of the Pope!

A few years earlier, however, the exclusivism that had long been assumed by most Christians had become church dogma. The Council of Florence, which met from 1438 to 1445, declared that "those not living within the Catholic Church, not only pagans, but also Jews and heretics and schismatics cannot become participants in eternal life, but will depart 'into the eternal fire prepared for the devil and his angels' [Matt. 25:41], unless before the end of life the same have been added to the flock."[7]

The church which could speak with such confidence of itself was on the threshold of inner division. The synthesis of classical and biblical modes of thinking through which it had conquered the pagan mind had long obscured the profound differences in its sources, but by the fifteenth century scholars were beginning to recover the distinct integrity of these sources and to contrast them with the medieval form of the synthesis. The Renaissance involved the celebration of pagan art and thought to the discredit of scholasticism. The Protestant reformers attacked scholasticism from the point of view of a new appreciation of the integrity of the biblical text.

This led to a heightened sense of the distinctively biblical faith and a depreciation of the Greek philosophy which had been interwoven with it. The reformers wanted to purify Christianity of the distortions introduced by assimilation of so much of pagan culture. In the process they developed a more negative attitude toward other religious Ways. They conceived the relation of Christian faith to these in terms of the contrast of divine revelation to human reason, or divine grace to human efforts at self-justification.

Luther emphasized that only revelation frees us from our endless human efforts to save ourselves through our works. Hence he and his followers had no reason to attend to other religions to observe the excellence of their thought or ethics. Calvin did not deny that something could be known of God through the world God created, but he emphasized the willful blindness of fallen human beings. Hence in the Calvinist tradition theologians did not look at other religious Ways in order to display their shared grasp of truth or their relative value and validity.

One might have thought that the renewal of distinctively biblical modes of thought purified of their interpretation through pagan philosophy would have made the reformers more appreciative of Judaism. Unfortunately, it did not. Luther in particular formulated Christian distinctiveness in terms of an extreme Christocentrism and contrasted Christianity as a religion of grace with Judaism as a religion of law. Since legalism is the supreme enemy of faith, hostility to Judaism was even intensified in Lutheranism. Luther's language about the Jews, especially as uttered toward the end of his life, is too vicious to bear repeating.

Although the Reformation, and to some extent also the Counter-Reformation, turned attention away from reason toward faith, the controversies engendered by competing forms of Christian faith led to a reaction. Reasonable people began seeking a *modus vivendi*, and this included the attempt to distinguish between the conflicting pronouncements of the various churches and the core of truth shared by them and all rational people. The idea arose that there is a natural religion expressed in, but also corrupted by, the positive religions.

In 1624 Lord Herbert of Cherbury published *De Veritate* and included a section on "Common Notions Concerning Religion." Here he argued that there are five notions innate to the human mind which are more or less adequately and purely expressed in all religions: "There is a supreme God." "This sovereign deity ought to be worshipped." "The connection of Virtue and Piety, defined in this work as the right conformation of the faculties, is and always has been held to be, the most important part of religious practice." "The minds of men have always been filled with horror for their wickedness." "Their vices and crimes have been obvious to them. They must be expiated by repentance." "There is Reward or Punishment after this Life."[8]

John Locke's critique of innate ideas shifted this rationalistic tradition toward a type of argument more like that of St. Thomas. Locke himself showed the reasonableness of basic religious beliefs, and others continued to argue for a form of religion common to all people, based on reason except as it has been distorted by selfish and perverse leaders.

For the most part this tradition developed with limited knowledge of the actual practices and beliefs of other religions but encounter with China served to give it support. The French Jesuit Philippe Couple translated Confucius in 1587, and the realization in Europe that a great civilization based on these rational, ethical, and religious teachings had endured for millennia strengthened the conviction that reason alone can provide an adequate ground for religion and ethics. Christian scholars took new interest in the Logos doctrine of the early church as a way of understanding and appreciating Confucian thought. The renewed appreciation of classical thinkers during the Renaissance also contributed to this climate of opinion. Voltaire saw in China the exemplification of the true religion of nature.

This tradition climaxed in the work of Immanuel Kant in *Religion Within the Limits of Reason Alone.*[9] For him, as for all those in this tradition, the norm for religion is given by a universal reason. It is assumed that this reason has operated in all religions, but that in their concrete manifestations it is to some degree concealed and distorted. The task is purification of all the actual historical Ways.

With G. W. F. Hegel there begins a new appreciation of the radically historical character of reason as well as religion. Both are parts of Spirit or *Geist* which is at once the divine principle and the truth or reality of the human mind. Hegel sees the history of *Geist* as a movement of civilization beginning in China and culminating in Protestant Europe.

Friedrich Schleiermacher also interpreted human religion in a historical and developmental way, perceiving its culmination in monotheism. But he, more than Hegel, recognized a plurality of parallel manifestations of this monotheism in Judaism, Islam, and Christianity. He then proceeded to describe the differences between these three monotheistic religions in such a way as to display the superiority of Christianity.

Although few follow Hegel and Schleiermacher in detail today, the patterns of their thought continue to be important. Hegel views all events in the context of universal history moving toward a consummation. This history is no longer simply the history of Israel and Christianity for these must be set in a wider context which includes the contributions of other civilizations. Hegel retained the linearity of sacred history, seeing *Geist* at work in one place and then moving on to another. This element does not hold up well in the light of historical study and conflicts with our understanding of religious pluralism, but the attempt to understand the relation of Christian faith to other Ways in the context of their several contributions to universal history continues to offer itself as a living option in our time.

Schleiermacher, on the other hand, proposed that we identify the religious *a priori*, that is, the universal element in human experience which distinguishes the religious from everything else. His proposal was that this is the feeling of absolute dependence. Subsequent thinkers have preferred to focus on the sense of the holy, on ultimate concern, or on the relation to the transcendent, but such changes do not alter the fundamental pattern. Once religion is defined in this way, individual religions are interpreted and evaluated as diverse modes of embodiment of this one essence or *a priori*. Christians have generally followed Schleiermacher in finding that the religious *a priori* has its purest and most adequate expression in Christianity, but by varying the definition of the religious essence, other Ways can make similar claims for themselves.

At the beginning of the twentieth century Ernst Troeltsch struggled with the legacy of Hegel and Schleiermacher in the light of the vastly increased knowledge of Asian traditions that was available to him. His hope and intention were to display the world-historical superiority of Christianity in its embodiment of the Spirit. He tried to show that the other great traditions were too closely bound to specific features of their cultures to offer the path to universal human fulfillment. But his further studies convinced him that Christianity was more culture-bound than he had thought and that the great religions of Asia were more culture-transcendent than he had recognized. He concluded that among the great religions each was adapted to the needs of its own culture and that there was no perspective from which questions of objective superiority could be responsibly raised. Thus Troeltsch became, reluctantly, the first great Christian relativist.

Kant, Hegel, and Schleiermacher all dealt with Christianity as a phenomenon which could be viewed from outside itself alongside other religious phenomena. Clearly the perspective from which Christianity was viewed was itself deeply influenced by Christianity in all three cases. And Schleiermacher understood theology itself as largely confessional. Nevertheless, viewed against the background of the Reformation, the effort of all three to appraise Christianity from an objective vantage point is striking.

This effort does not characterize all nineteenth-century Christian thinkers. Kierkegaard and Ritschl did not have a comparable interest in other religious Ways. Their understanding of Christian theology was more fully confessional and dogmatic.

This alternative tradition blossomed in the work of the greatest of twentieth-century theologians, Karl Barth. He did not reject religion entirely or deny that Christianity has religious aspects, but he did reject the effort to understand Christianity as one historical phenomenon alongside others, at least as a basis for Christian affirmations. Christian faith is response to the unique act of God in the incarnation, and Christian dogmatics is the human effort faithfully to acknowledge that act and to understand it. Hence the Christian task is not to argue the respective merits of

Christianity and other religious Ways but to witness to the uniquely salvific event in which God acted once for all for human salvation. This event is incommensurate with any other. It contains its own criteria and cannot be judged or evaluated from any other point of view. This does not mean, however, that salvation is the exclusive possession of Christians. On the contrary, God's act in Jesus Christ was for all. Christians witness to a salvation already effected for everyone.

Barth's form of confessional theology radically overcame the relativity of faith to culture with which Troeltsch had concluded his study, but it did so by removing Jesus Christ from human history. There were others, however, who believed that confessional theology could proceed best by deepening the awareness of historical relativity and our inevitable immersion in it rather than by finding in the incarnation the Archimedean point of transcendence. H. Richard Niebuhr's book on *The Meaning of Revelation* provides the classic formulation for this quite different style of theology.[10]

Niebuhr believed that there is no escape from the relativity into which we are cast by history—and no need for escape. Our task is to recognize that we are conditioned by our history in every fiber of our being. But this does not mean that we are simply the products of objective events. At a deeper level, we live by an inner history of meaning. Christians are those who live by an inner history in which the memory of Jesus Christ is the illuminating and determinative center of our corporate and personal lives. This inner history of meaning cannot be proved true or false, good or bad, by some objective standard, but we can and should confess how it appears true and good to us. Such confession, however, is in no way incompatible with listening to others as they tell us their stories of inner history and witness to the meaning and value they find through these stories. In this way Niebuhr points through relativism to pluralism.

Five major patterns have emerged from this survey which appear to be relevant to the task of Christian theology in a time of appreciative awareness of other religious Ways. One comes from the ancient church. This is the Logos Christology, the chief doctrine through which the church was able to appropriate so much wisdom from the Greeks. The other four have been described in this section in terms of universal history, the religious *a priori*, dogmatic confession, and pluralistic confession. Rationalism and thoroughgoing relativism fall outside the boundaries of Christian theology, and an exclusivistic view that sees no salvific work outside the boundaries of explicit Christian faith is today widely felt as unacceptable, despite its importance in much of the Christian tradition.

II. The Ecumenical Movement and Vatican II

The nineteenth century was a great age of Christian missions. On the whole, however, these missions were little concerned with the positive values of the religious traditions of the people to whom they were directed. A few missionaries did study these traditions, but most could proceed to the conversion of the heathen without this concern. It was generally taken for granted that the success of the Christian mission would mean the supplanting of whatever had preceded it.

As late as the occasion of the First World Missionary Conference at Edinburgh in 1910, missionary strategists anticipated the disintegration of the non-Christian religions and their supersession by Christianity. The climactic statement of Julius Richter's inaugural address at Berlin expresses the characteristic vision. "Mission apologetics is that branch of theology which in opposition to the non-Christian religions, shows the Christian religion to be the Way, the Truth and the Life; which seeks to dispossess the non-Christian religions and to plant in their stead in the soil of heathen national life the evangelic faith and the Christian life."[11]

By 1928, when the Second World Missionary Conference convened in Jerusalem, however, the situation had changed. Missionaries recognized something positive in the resurgence of traditional Asian religions. Secularism appeared as a greater threat to Christianity than did heathenism. There was talk of a common front of the world's religions against atheism.

Among thoughtful lay people in the United States seeds of doubt about the need to convert the heathen had been planted by the World Parliament of Religions in 1893 where the Hindu thinker and mystic, Vivekananda, made a profound impression. Finally, in 1930 a group of lay people organized a commission to evaluate the work of Christian mission. The report favored the continuation of mission, but it stressed the importance of appreciation of other religious Ways. "The mission of today should make a positive effort first of all to know and understand the religions around it, then to recognize and associate itself with whatever kindred elements there are."[12] The chairman of the commission, William Ernest Hocking, accented this element in his introductory section on general principles. He argued that all religions share a fundamental religious intuition, hence they can help one another in the quest for fuller religious truth, and they can work together to check the rising tide of secularism. Hocking developed his ideas further in lectures at Oxford and Cambridge in 1936.

Hocking found the essence of religion in "a passion for righteousness, and for the spread of righteousness, conceived as a cosmic demand."[13] In the encounter of religions each can grasp its own essence better and, through that improved understanding, also become more inclusive of what others have attained. This is the process of reconception. Its implementation calls for institutions to promote what has subsequently been known as dialogue to supplement existing forms of mission. In Hocking's words: "The mission is set for teaching; the required institution must be set for learning as well. The mission is set for the announcement of doctrine; this institution must be set for conversation and conference. The mission is set for activity; this institution must be set also for leisure, contemplation, study."[14]

This move toward pluralism set the challenge of the Third World Missionary Conference at Madras, or Tambaram, in 1938. In response to Hocking, Hendrick Kraemer wrote for this conference *The Christian Message in a Non-Christian World.*[15] Kraemer rejected the view that all religions have the same essence. The realistic biblical perspective grounded in revelation is unique and discontinuous with all other perspectives. Like Barth, Kraemer recognized that Christianity, too, is a religion, with all the weaknesses and failures of religion. But the revelation of God in Jesus Christ stands beyond the relativities of religion.

Kraemer believed that biblical realism and the cores of other religions deal with the same totality of existence. In this respect they are more comparable than in Barth's view. Far more than Barth, he has been concerned to study each religion in its individual particularity and to analyze its strengths and weaknesses from the point of view of revelation. Whereas the major emphasis of *The Christian Message in a Non-Christian World* was the negation of other religions, he subsequently wrote *Religion and the Christian Faith* to express his appreciation of the positive achievements of other religions.[16] Nevertheless, these do not abolish the fundamental distinction between revelation and religion or overcome the discontinuity between Christian faith and the other religions.

The Tambaram Conference was deeply affected by Kraemer's work and adopted his general stance as its own. Nevertheless, there was division of opinion on one crucial point. "As to whether the non-Christian religions as total systems of thought and life may be in some sense or to some degree manifestating God's revelation, Christians are not agreed."[17]

Although the Tambaram Conference turned away from approaching the resurgent religious movements of Asia as partners embodying the same religious essence, it did not close the door to continuing study of and contact with them. During the years after World War II the rising self-confidence of Asian cultures and religions continued to press for attention from Christians. It was imperative that Christians work together with others in nation-building. The International Missionary Council and the World Council of Churches established a joint study in 1955 on "The Word of God and the Living Faiths of Men." In *Religion and the Christian Faith*, published soon thereafter, Kraemer recognized the "coming dialogue" between East and West as the significant framework of Christian mission. In the reorganization of the World Council of Churches in 1971 the Programme Unit on Faith and Witness was structured into four subunits: Faith and Order, Church and Society, World Mission and Evangelism, and Dialogue with People of Living Faiths and Ideologies. The WCC affirmed the importance and even the necessity of dialogue for the church and called for particular attention to dialogue with the traditional religions of Africa.

The inclusion of "and ideologies" in the title of the subunit is noteworthy. It reflects debate during the sixties with respect to the Christian stance toward religious traditions on the one side and secularity on the other. The Jerusalem Conference and the Laymen's Report in the period between the World Wars had called for religious unity to oppose secularism. On the other hand, the Barthian critique of religion led in the sixties to the call for an alliance between Christianity and secular movements and forces against what A. T. van Leeuwen called "ontocratic cultures."[18] Although this point of view did not entirely carry the day, the Central Committee of the WCC meeting on Crete in 1967 decreed: "In order that the context of dialogue may not be limited to the common acceptance of religious presuppositions, it is important that exponents of Marxist or humanistic atheism should be drawn into multilateral dialogue."[19]

Despite the acceptance of dialogue as a major program emphasis of the World Council of Churches, the theological grounds for dialogue are still undeveloped. This is because of a tension between two basic Christian positions. One group, and this includes many of those who participate most actively in dialogue with persons of other faiths, takes the religious convictions of these persons with great seriousness and wants to understand them better. For these Christians, dialogue is a profound spiritual sharing on the basis of full mutuality between religious movements.

This makes good sense from the point of view of the Jerusalem Conference, the Laymen's Report, and Hocking's proposals. But it is not acceptable from the point of view of Barth, Kraemer, and the Tambaram Conference. For this other group, there cannot be full mutuality between, for example, Christians as Christians and Muslims as Muslims. That is, the Christian cannot view what the Muslim has to say about Muslim beliefs as on a par with the Christian witness to the act of God in Jesus Christ, and Christians cannot be interested in religious sharing as such. Hence the mutuality essential for dialogue must be *human* mutuality. Although much, probably most, of the actual dialogue is carried out by persons in the first group, the official justification can only be expressed in a way that commands the assent of the second.

Both positions are expressed in World Council of Churches literature. The former is found in the guidelines for interreligious dialogue proposed by Stanley Samartha, director of the unit on Dialogue with People of Living Faiths and Ideologies. Samartha states that "the basis of inter-religious dialogue is the *commitment* of all partners to their respective faiths and their *openness* to the insights of the others. The integrity of particular religions must be recognised." The dialogue "must lead to the enrichment of all in the discovery of new dimensions of Truth." And it "should also stress the need to study *fundamental questions* in the religious dimension of life."[20]

This position is supported in the report of the 1967 Kandy consultation on Christians in Dialogue with Men of Other Faiths. This consultation brought together Protestant, Orthodox, and Catholic thinkers especially concerned with inter-religious dialogue. Their conclusion was that since the Christian "must take seriously the personalities of his neighbors, he must of course respect their particular religious faith as an integral aspect of their culture and humanity. As our dialogue with men of other faiths develops, we may gain light regarding the place held by other religious traditions in God's purposes for them and for us."[21] It entails "a positive effort to attain a deeper understanding of the truth through mutual awareness of one another's convictions and witness."[22] Both the guidelines and this statement clearly take the religious conviction of the dialogue partner with full seriousness.

The second position dominated the Uppsala assembly the following year. The account of dialogue in the draft prepared for discussion at Uppsala states that the Christian "must listen to artists and scientists, to men of other faiths, and to agnostics, to learn what news Christ has for him through them."[23] Here we are listening to persons as persons without explicit reference to the religious dimension of their concern. The final report states that "each meets and challenges the other; witnessing from the depths of his existence to the ultimate concerns that come to expression in word and action."[24] This acknowledges that there is a depth to all human beings which cannot be neglected in authentic dialogue. It does not suggest that this depth is something shared in particular by persons of religious faith.[25]

Thus, although those most closely involved in dialogue are often motivated by a primary interest in understanding and relating to the dialogue partners as representatives of other religious traditions, the theoretical justification of the dialogue does not support that interest. It directs attention more properly to shared concern for nation-building and for world community. Also, whereas Stanley Samartha, the first director of the subunit, had a more positive view of other religions than that which controls the official statements, his emphasis was not on the confrontation of different doctrines but on personal understanding. In explaining the theological reasons for dialogue he writes: "there is the promise of Jesus Christ that the Holy Spirit will lead us into all truth. Since truth, in the biblical understanding, is not propositional but relational, and is to be sought, not in the isolation of lonely meditation, but in the living, personal confrontation between God and man, and men and men, dialogue becomes one of the means of the quest for truth. And because Christians cannot claim to have a monopoly of truth, we need to meet men of other faiths and ideologies as part of our trust in and obedience to the promise of Christ."[26]

It is therefore understandable that when a section of a WCC assembly was devoted to questions of dialogue for the first time—at Nairobi in 1975—the section was entitled "Seeking Community." The discussions in this section dealt primarily with the need for inclusive community and how Christians may work with others to attain it. Nevertheless, the fact that the section report referred to sharing in spirituality led to the charge that it was dangerously close to syncretism by failing to maintain the radical difference between the gospel and religion. As a result the final report repudiated syncretism, which it defined as "conscious or unconscious attempts to create a new religion composed of elements from different religions."[27]

The tension between the two groups could be lessened if it could be acknowledged that "the non-Christian religions as total systems of thought and life may be regarded as in some sense or to some degree manifesting God's revelation."[28] But as at Tambaram, Christians continued to find that they do not agree. In an effort to work through some of the issues left unsettled at Nairobi, a consultation was called on the nature and purpose of dialogue in community at Chiang Mai in 1977. But once again the important questions of the relationship of God's universal action in creation to God's redemptive action in Jesus Christ were left unsettled. Meanwhile the WCC continues to sponsor consultations with people of other faiths on matters of common concern.[29]

Despite the strong emphasis on listening in dialogue, it is not clear just what Christians are expected to learn. In 1971 the Central Committee issued "An Interim Policy Statement and Guidelines" on "The WCC and Dialogue with People of Living Faiths and Ideologies." They affirmed that "dialogue offers the promise of discovering new dimensions of understanding our faith."[30] They also saw that dialogue is useful for purposes of establishing the faith in non-Christian cultures. The statement asks but does not answer the question of the fundamental theological implications of dialogue. Earlier a consultation at Zurich, reflecting on the meaning of an important multireligious conversation at Ibadan, spoke in its *Aide-memoire* in stronger terms: "Dialogue thus involves the risk of one partner being changed by the other."[31] It "implies a readiness to receive an enrichment and enlargement."[32] But this more radical conception of dialogue has not been taken up into subsequent WCC discussions. The World Council of Churches promotes dialogues, but it has not yet succeeded in clarifying their purpose.

While Protestants and Orthodox developed their positions through WCC discussion, the Roman Catholic position long seemed to remain static, but once the question of other religions was reopened officially in Roman Catholic thought, the church moved much faster and more clearly than the WCC had been able to do. The Vatican Council adopted *Nostra Aetate*, a decree specifically on the subject of other religions. Comments about the other religions were brief but uniformly positive in tone.

Like the WCC the decree begins by affirming common humanity as the basis for community with non-Christians. However, unlike the dominant tradition in the WCC, the Catholic church views religion positively. The religious experience and faith found outside of Christianity express "the truth which enlightens every man."[33] Hence Christians confront other religious traditions in which they find both truth and value.

Read together with other Council documents this means that salvation can also be realized in other religious communities. In *Lumen Gentium* it is affirmed that God provides saving grace to all who honestly seek it. There are even suggestions of a history of salvation in which all the religions have some role to play.

During Vatican II Pope Paul VI announced the establishment of a Secretariat for Non-Christian Religions. In his first encyclical letter he included a call for a *colloquium salutis*, a dialogue on salvation, to be pursued with persons of good will, including followers of other religious traditions. The clear implication is that these traditions also know something of salvation.

One week after the Council approved the Declaration on Non-Christian Religions a conference was held in Bombay on "Christian Revelation and Non-Christian Religions." Some of the papers presented there disturbed the Council fathers for their exploitation of the new possibilities opened up by the Council. Among these the most important was that of Hans Küng.

Küng moves radically in the direction of history of salvation. He argues that God in Christ is in fact at work everywhere seeking human salvation and that he makes use of all of the world's religions to effect salvation. In his words: "1. *Every* human being is under God's grace and can be saved: whether he be of this or that nation or race, of this or that caste or class, free or slave, man or woman, or even inside or outside the Church of Christ. Every human being can be saved, and we may hope that everyone is. 2. Every world religion is under God's grace and can be a way of salvation: whether it is primitive or highly evolved, mythological or enlightened, mystical or rational, theistic or non-theistic, a real or only a quasi-religion. Every religion can be a way of salvation, and we may hope that every one is."[34] This does not mean, however, that religions are unambiguously good. Indeed, Küng emphasizes the profound errors which infect them, especially the error in not discerning the truth which they express. But the task of Christianity is not so much to convert individuals from these religions as to serve the religions as such. Christianity is the sign of what they are destined to become.

This proposal disturbed the bishops at the Council. Although they taught that there is salvation outside the church, they believed that there was no salvation apart from the church. Further, they intended to affirm the Christian witness to individuals with the intention of incorporating them into the Christian community. Hallencreutz notes that "this controversy had effects on the deliberations during the final session of the Council. Compared with *Lumen Gentium 16*, *Ad Gentes 7* was more restrained in its recognition even of the possibility of attaining salvation outside the Church."[35]

The church leadership was more ready to follow the careful and cautious thought of Karl Rahner. He introduced the idea of the "anonymous Christian"[36] as the person who unknowingly received the grace of Christ outside the church. For Rahner, as for Küng, the non-Christian religions can play a positive role in making this grace available to their believers. But for him, when the Christian church arrives on the scene, the need for these other traditions is in principle superseded.

Although the idea of anonymous Christians has been widely employed in Catholic circles, it has also been sharply criticized. Küng, for one, finds it arrogant to impose the category of Christian on those who do not want it.[37]

Official responsibility for clarifying and implementing the decisions of the Council falls upon the new Secretariat for Non-Christian Religions. This secretariat has cooperated closely with the WCC unit on Dialogue with People of Living Faiths and Ideologies, but its mandate is different and leads to different patterns of research. Its task is to effect dialogue on the subject of salvation with representatives of other religious traditions. This requires both that the Catholic participants in the dialogue understand the position from which they discuss and also that they learn more about what is understood by salvation in other traditions.

The position taken by the secretariat is expressed in an important statement by Cardinal Pietro Rossano. "By means of the announcement of the word of God and the exercise of her ministry, she [the Church] brings salvation to all men, who may, if they live uprightly, though they do not know the Church, participate in the salvation of God and of Christ even outside the visible membership of the Church, but not without her."[38]

As applied to dialogue with individual religious traditions such as Islam, Rossano's position leads to the implication that Muslims can achieve salvation by means of Islam. The Christian can discern certain limitations of Islam and can hope through dialogue to offer what Islam lacks, for example, a certain intimacy with God. But both Islam and Christianity are seen within the total history of salvation: "That divine pedagogy, which in mysterious ways causes such different sorts of people to progress towards the fullness of God's gift to man."[39]

The insistence that salvation occurs outside the church and apart from the confession of Christ has been even more emphatic in the utterances of Pope John Paul II. In his initial speech as pope, *Redemptor Hominis*, he quoted the Second Vatican Council's *Gaudium et Spes* as follows: "by His incarnation the Son of God . . . united himself in some fashion with every man."[40] The pope expanded this idea forcefully. "The human person—every person without exception—has been redeemed by Christ; because Christ is in a way united to the human person—every person without exception—even if the individual may not realize this fact. Christ, who died and was raised up for all—for every human being and for all human beings—can through his spirit offer man the light and the strength to measure up to his supreme destiny!"[41] John Paul II reiterated in the same address the high esteem in which the church holds other religious movements.

Even so, it is not clear whether, from this Catholic point of view, Christians have anything important to gain from dialogue. The emphasis is on what we have to contribute to others. Cardinal Morella, the first director of the Secretariat for Non-Christian Religions, expressed the hope of regaining insights through the dialogue which Christians had lost or obscured during the course of history, but he did not envisage that there is any limitation in the religion of Christ which is to be completed through dialogue. On the other hand, in 1979 Cardinal Rossano, the current director, concluded his address to a North American gathering on "Christ's Lordship and Religious Pluralism" with these words: "This is why the Christian's attitude to the religions of the world is one of humility and respect, and of frankness in giving witness to Christ, the Word that enlightens every person, *paratus semper nuntiare, paratus semper doceri,* always ready to announce, always ready to be taught."[42] Nevertheless, even in this speech the acceptance of full reciprocity remains muted. The emphasis in on the perfecting of other religious traditions.

NOTES

1. Irenaeus, *Adversus Haereses,* III: 12,13.
2. Augustine, *Epistola,* 102:12.
3. Robert Lawson Slater, *Can Christians Learn from Other Religions?* (New York: Seabury Press, 1963), p.13. Slater is quoting Basil of Caesarea.
4. Arnoldo Momigliano, "Pagan and Christian Historiography in the Fourth Century A.D.," in *The Conflict between Paganism and Christianity in the Fourth Century,* ed. Arnoldo Momigliano (Oxford: Clarendon Press, 1963), p. 87.
5. Tertullian, *De Praescriptione Haeriticum,* vii.
6. Nicholas of Cusa, "De Pace Fidei," *Unity and Reform: Selected Writings of Nicholas de Cusa,* ed. John Patrick Dolan (Notre Dame, Indiana: University of Notre Dame Press, 1962).
7. Heinrich Denzinger, *The Sources of Catholic Dogma* [Enchiridion Symbolorum] trans. Roy J. Deferrari from the 30th ed. (St. Louis: Herder, 1957), p. 230.
8. Edward Herbert Herbert (Lord Herbert of Cherbury) *De Veritate,* trans. Myrick Carré (Bristol: J. W. Arrowsmith, 1937).
9. Immanuel Kant, *Religion Within the Limits of Reason Alone* (Chicago: Open Court Publishing Co., 1934).
10. H. Richard Niebuhr, *The Meaning of Revelation* (New York: Macmillan, 1941).
11. Julius Richter, "Missionary Apologetic: Its Problem and Its Methods," *International Review of Missions* 2 (1913): 540.
12. Laymen's Foreign Missions Inquiry, Commission of Appraisal,

Rethinking Mission: A Laymen's Inquiry after 100 Years (New York: Harper & Bros., 1932), pp. 326–27.

13. William Ernest Hocking, *Living Religions and a World Faith* (New York: Macmillan, 1940), p. 26.

14. Ibid., p. 205

15. Hendrik Kraemer, *The Christian Message in a Non-Christian World* (London: Harper & Bros., 1938).

16. Hendrik Kraemer, *Religion and the Christian Faith* (Philadelphia: Westminster Press, 1957).

17. *The Authority of Faith,* The Madras Series (New York: International Missionary Council, 1939) 1: 194.

18. A. T. van Leeuwen, *Christianity in World History: The Meeting of the Faiths of East and West,* trans. H. H. Hoskins (London: Edinburgh House Press, 1964), p. 165 and passim.

19. World Council of Churches Central Committee, *Minutes and Reports of the Twentieth Meeting. Heraklion, Crete, Greece* (Geneva: World Council of Churches, 1967), p. 190.

20. Stanley Samartha, "The Progress and Promise of Inter-Religious Dialogues," *Journal of Ecumenical Studies* 9 (1972): 473–74.

21. "Christians in Dialogue with Men of Other Faiths," *International Review of Missions* 56 (1967): 339.

22. Ibid., pp. 339–40.

23. World Council of Churches, 4th Assembly, Uppsala, 1968, *Drafts for Sections: Prepared for the Fourth Assembly of the World Council of Churches, Uppsala, Sweden, 1968* (Geneva: World Council of Churches, 1968), p. 29.

24. World Council of Churches, 4th Assembly, Uppsala, 1968, *The Uppsala Report 1968* (Geneva: World Council of Churches, 1968), p. 29.

25. I am indebted for the material in these two paragraphs, as well as for help elsewhere, to two books by Carl F. Hallencreutz: *New Approaches to Men of Other Faiths: 1938–1968* (Geneva: World Council of Churches, 1970) and *Dialogue and Community: Ecumenical Issues in Inter-Religious Relationships* (Uppsala, Sweden: Swedish Institute of Missionary Research, 1977).

26. Stanley Samartha, "Dialogue as a Continuing Christian Concern," in *Living Faiths and the Ecumenical Movement,* ed. Stanley Samartha (Geneva: World Council of Churches, 1971), pp. 153–54. Also in John Hick and Brian Hebblethwaite, eds., *Christianity and Other Religions* (Philadelphia: Fortress Press, 1980).

27. Hallencreutz, *Dialogue and Community,* p. 100.

28. *The Authority of Faith,* p. 194.

29. A preliminary inquiry by Christians and Buddhists into the religious dimensions in humanity's relation to nature was held at Colombo in 1978. See S. J. Samartha and D. Lynn de Silva, eds., *Man in Nature:*

Guest or Engineer (Colombo: The Ecumenical Institute for Study and Dialogue, 1979), p. 50.

30. Samartha, *Living Faiths and the Ecumenical Movement*, p. 50.

31. Ibid., p. 34.

32. Ibid., p. 42.

33. See "Declaration on the Relation of the Church to Non Christian Religions, Vatican II, *Nostra Aetate*, 28 Oct. 1965," in *Vatican Council II: The Conciliar and Post Conciliar Documents*, ed. Austin Flannery, trans. Fr. Killian (Collegeville, Minnesota: Liturgical Press, 1975), pp. 738–42.

34. Hans Küng, "The World Religions in God's Plan of Salvation," in *Christian Revelation and World Religions*, ed. Joseph Neuner (London: Burns & Oates, 1967) cited in *Attitudes towards Other Religions: Some Christian Interpretations*, ed. Owen C. Thomas (New York: Harper & Row, 1969), p. 216.

35. Hallencreutz, *Dialogue and Community*, 50.

36. Karl Rahner has used this term at least since 1961. See "Christianity and the Non-Christian Religions," constituting notes of a lecture given on April 28, 1961 in Eichstätt (Bavaria) and published in *Theological Investigations*, vol. 5. (New York: Seabury Press, 1966).

37. Hans Küng, *On Being a Christian*, trans. Edward Quine (Garden City, New York: Doubleday & Co., 1976), p. 98.

38. *Religions* (Rome: Marella Ed., 1970), cited in Hallencreutz, *Dialogue and Community*, p. 69.

39. *Guidelines for a Dialogue between Muslims and Christians* (Rome, 1969) pp. 135–37, cited in Hallencreutz, *Dialogue and Community*, p. 70.

40. John Paul II, "The Redeemer of the Human Race," *The Pope Speaks* 24 (1979): 115.

41. Ibid., p. 118.

42. Pietro Rossano, "A Roman Catholic Perspective," in *Christ's Lordship and Religious Pluralism*, ed. Gerald H. Anderson and Thomas F. Stransky (Maryknoll, N.Y.: Orbis Books, 1981), p. 109.

CHAPTER TWO

The Road Through Dialogue and Beyond

Chapter One traced the history of Christian interpretation of other religious Ways to the point at which dialogue became, for both the WCC and the Roman Catholic church, a major imperative. It presented the theoretical grounds for dialogue as officially expressed in the two communities. It noted that on the Protestant side the practice of dialogue often expresses a theological stance different from that which is dominant in the WCC. This chapter will begin by surveying positions of individual Catholic and Protestant theologians which develop or diverge from those that have gained official support.

The second section of the chapter shifts from historical survey and summary of the positions of others to argument. The purpose of this book is to put forward a constructive proposal, and this will begin with critical evaluation of the positions of others and proceed to draw positive conclusions.

I. Beyond the Official Positions

The way in which the thinking of the Catholic church develops is through the interaction of creative individual theologians and the authoritative teaching of popes and councils. Vatican II could not have taken place apart from the original work of many theologians exploring the meaning of earlier Catholic teaching in relation to a changing world situation. The task of Catholic theologians since Vatican II has been to clarify and develop the ideas formulated there. Already Chapter One took note of the relation of the thought of Hans Küng and Karl Rahner to the Council and its aftermath.

Although Vatican II did not specifically assert that the other religions are means of salvation, it was open to this interpretation.

Hans Küng, Karl Rahner, and the Vatican Secretariat for Non-Christian Religions have all adopted this doctrine. In the ongoing Catholic discussion, this is a major, though still disputed, position. According to Paul Knitter, indeed, it follows from the Catholic understanding of religion not only that all religions possess "elements of goodness and truth" as the Council affirmed, but also that they are legitimate ways of salvation.[1] This means that Catholics can follow Küng in understanding the Christian mission to be one of service to the religions rather than proselytizing among their adherents. Nevertheless, most Catholic theologians continue to teach that Christianity is not only a true religion but also the absolute one, the one to which all others must finally move, and Knitter shows that the problems caused by this doctrine have moved to the center of discussion.

Criticisms of this claim arise partly because of its offensiveness to many Catholics in the ongoing life and practice of the church. Our concern here, however, is with its effects on dialogue with outsiders. There is a fundamental tension between the imperative to dialogue and the insistence on already possessing the one absolute religion. This insistence implies that Christians have fundamentally nothing to learn from their dialogue partners, but as Donald Swearer points out,

> one of the first requisites for a dialogue . . . is the necessity of *being engaged by the faith of the other.* Nothing significant emerges out of dialogue unless we have been seriously tested, challenged, and enticed by the faith stance of our partners in dialogue. If we approach people of other religious persuasions purely from the standpoint of advocacy, if we believe that our particular perception of religious truth is the *only* correct one, then genuine dialogue does not take place. What occurs is merely a series of monologues.[2]

Even when the absolutist stance is combined with the recognition of the salvific efficacy of other religions, it encourages the assumption that Christian faith is the one final destiny in which the others can be fulfilled. Most Catholic theologians continue to hold to that position. Paul Knitter writes: "In describing how the world religions are . . . related to Christianity, these theologians present the religions as 'advent forms', 'previews' *(Vorentwürfe)*, 'pathfinders' *(Wegbereiter)*, carrying out a role similar to the Old Testament; or as Vatican II phrases it, the religions are a *praeparatio evangelica* in which the 'presence of God' is only 'secret', to be revealed in 'the fulness of religious life' found in Christianity."[3] On the other side, Chapter One noted that the preparatory materials for dialogue with Muslims did not assume only a temporary role for Islam. And M. Zago writes: "The Church has the duty to be a sign and sacrament of salvation to the whole of mankind: it should help Buddhism progress along its own course of the history of salvation, and in a way work to make the Buddhist a better Buddhist."[4] H. Maurier also protests that "if Christianity is the definitive truth, the absoluteness of God's revelation to mankind, it only remains for the other religions to convert to Christianity. . . . What we have, in fact, is a dialogue between the elephant and the mouse."[5]

Maurier goes on to make a second equally important point. For him it would be insufficient to recognize only that other religions have a place in the history of salvation that is not necessarily superseded by Christianity. It would be important also to recognize the integrity of the ways in which this process of salvation is understood in each tradition. If we believe that Christ is ultimately the only savior, then "even if we recognise that men are saved in and by their successive religions, . . . we are still envisaging the other religions from within the absoluteness of Christianity; fundamentally, the other religion is none the less disqualified. And, in every fibre of its being, it refuses to be disqualified."[6]

Agreeing with Maurier, Knitter proposes that Catholic theology shift from Christocentrism to theocentrism. What Christians "wished to proclaim for themselves and the world was that in Jesus we encounter the Christ; in him we are challenged by a full, a true, a reliable revelation of the saving God, a revelation which is relevant for all peoples of all times."[7] This absoluteness of the revelation demands a total commitment and is in this sense absolute, but it "does not rule out the possibility of recognizing other absolutes. . . . Total commitment to one's own particular Revealer is *not* exclusive of total openness to the universal God in other particular Revealers. Such an attitude is, it seems, a *conditio sine qua non* for authentic religion and authentic religious dialogue."[8] This approach enables

> Christians to realise ever more clearly that . . . Christianity's true revelation does not exhaust the Absolute and therefore must be related to and balanced by other, seemingly contrary, true revelations. . . . The Christian doctrine of the Trinity *needs* Islamic insistence on divine Oneness; the impersonal Emptiness of Buddhism needs the Christian experience of the divine Thou; the Christian teaching on the distinction between the Ultimate and the finite needs the Hindu insight into the Non-Duality between Brahman and Atman; the prophetic-praxis oriented content of the Judaeo-Christian tradition needs the Eastern stress on personal contemplation and "acting without seeking the fruits of action."[9]

This Catholic readiness for Christians to be changed through dialogue, a note almost absent from the official World Council of Churches pronouncements, is found among individual Protestant participants in the ecumenical discussions as well. The Methodist bishop, James K. Matthews, writes: "An unseemly anxiety to preserve our heritage is to lose it and, at the same time, to attempt to limit God; but a willingness finally to risk even the loss of our heritage in the service of God and man is to find it. When there is a readiness to risk at all, God may be trusted to be faithful in giving all back again in a renewed and enlarged perspective."[10]

A major leader in the WCC discussions, Stephen Neill, insists that one who has recognized Jesus "as the truth of God" cannot abandon this and remain a Christian, but he also recognizes that a Christian can and should "put himself to school" with other faiths "in readiness to believe that they may have something to teach him."[11] More recently he argued that as a result of dialogue faith is tested, purified, modified, and strengthened.[12] For him the first great task that now confronts the Christian churches is a deeper engagement with the non-Christian faiths.[13]

Another WCC leader, Bishop Leslie Newbigin, emphasizes the importance of receiving as well as giving in dialogue. He recognizes that this involves change on the Christian's part. Indeed, "much of his 'Christianity' may have to be left behind in this meeting. Much of the intellectual construction, the piety, the practice in which his discipleship of Christ has been expressed may have to be called in question."[14] For Newbigin this is fully compatible with commitment to the finality of Jesus Christ.[15]

While the World Council of Churches moved into dialogue with people of other faiths and debated whether this required openness to change in Christian belief, some of the leading Protestant theologians took up the discussion of the nature of Christian theology in its relation to the history of religions. After Troeltsch the two disciplines had parted company. Thinkers such as Rudolf Otto and Friedrich Heiler continued to hold them together in their own thought, but Paul Tillich comments sadly on their isolation.[16] Although Tillich never turned his back on the history of religions altogether, he addressed his major work, and especially his *Systematic Theology,* to the relation of Christian faith to the Western secular mind. However, in the eighth decade of his life he travelled to Japan and engaged in dialogue there with Buddhists. This experience led him to devote much of his last years to reflection on the relation of Christianity to other world religions. After a two-year joint seminar with Mircea Eliade and only a few days before his death, Tillich gave a programmatic lecture on "The Significance of the History of Religions for the Systematic Theologian."

Tillich's proposal was that theologians interpret Christianity once again in the context of the whole global phenomenon of religion. Strictly speaking it is not the *history* of religions but the *phenomenology* of religion which especially illumines Christian faith. He favored a "dynamic-typological" approach.[17] He judged that all religions have a sacramental base and also mystical and prophetic elements. When these elements are appropriately unified the result is "the Religion of the Concrete Spirit,"[18] which he connects with his earlier category of theonomy.[19] This provides a norm by which all actual religions can be evaluated. Tillich believed that this norm was fulfilled in Paul's doctrine of the Spirit.

During the period in which Tillich was turning to these questions, the brilliant younger theologian Wolfhart Pannenberg was also doing so. In 1962 he gave a lecture entitled "Toward a Theology of the History of Religions." Pannenberg means *history* and argues against the phenomenological and typological approach for one that takes seriously the actual course of events in the many religions of the world. Indeed, Pannenberg's most distinctive contribution to the discussion is the unqualifiedly historical approach which he affirms and adopts.

Pannenberg notes that religions have always interacted competitively with one another. Gods have assimilated other gods and taken over their functions. This sometimes goes with the victory of the worshipers of one god over the worshipers of another, but not always. Occasionally the god of the vanquished displays itself as religiously superior and is worshiped by the victors. But the victorious gods are transformed through their incorporation of the others.

Competition among the gods expresses the element of universality that is present in all religious claims. Today for the first time we live in a situation in which religion is truly universal as worshipers of all the gods interact. All are changed in this process, but throughout history many religions, despite their actual changes, have not been able to acknowledge change. They have been committed to a past or primordial manifestation of deity in such a way that they must always regard themselves as bound to that. The Bible, on the contrary, affirms historical change and points to the future as the locus of complete truth and knowledge. "Nevertheless, Israel continued to seek the fundamental revelation of its God in the events of the past. . . . It was Jesus who first turned this relationship around, departing from the religious traditions of his people where it seemed necessary to do so for the sake of the coming reign of God."[20] "As the power of the future, the God of the coming reign of God proclaimed by Jesus already anticipates all later epochs of the history of the church and of the non-Christian religions. From this standpoint, the history of religions even beyond the time of the public ministry of Jesus presents itself as a history of the appearance of the God who revealed himself through Jesus."[21]

This interpretation of the history of religions allows Pannenberg to see the one God as revealed in all religions and appraise them positively. Christians can learn from past and present religions and be transformed by what they learn. Indeed it is their thematic openness to that transformation and that alone which is their advantage in relation to others. Christians can learn from others and affirm that what they learn is about the God of Jesus. Others are in fact changed by their encounter with Christians and with one another, but they are inhibited by their understanding of their gods from recognizing the new elements in their lives as from those gods. The future belongs to the God of the Future.

Both Tillich and Pannenberg stood outside the kerygmatic theology that dominated the theological scene during the sixties and is still strong today. They hold that for the sake of dealing responsibly with other religions that style of theology must be rejected. Certainly its adherents have been slow to break the Barthian taboo against taking religions seriously.

Recently, however, Jürgen Moltmann, taking his stand essentially in the Barthian tradition, has called for radical openness to and in dialogue with other religions. He argues that the criticism of religion in the kerygmatic tradition was not directed to the other religions. The kerygmatic tradition saw "religion as the self-assertion of man."[22] "Its Christian criticism of religion was directed against the Christianity which has become 'religious' in this sense, not against the world religions. For that reason we cannot deduce the absolutism of Christianity over against the world religions from the theological difference between revelation and religion, faith and superstition. . . . The criticism of religion is directed on a quite different level to everyone, whether he be Christian, Jew, Moslem or Hindu."[23]

Christianity renounces all exclusive claims for itself. This includes Pannenberg's claim that it is God known in Jesus Christ who is the God of the Future. Moltmann is satisfied to allow the plurality of religions to remain. The goal is not the subsumption of all religions in Christianity but the genesis of a universal community in which all people are liberated. To this end Moltmann does not oppose the continued quantitative expansion of the Christian church, but he is more interested in "the qualitative alteration of life's atmosphere—of trust, feelings, thinking and acting. We might call this missionary aim to 'infect' people, whatever their religion, with the spirit of hope, love and responsibility for the world."[24] This "mission takes place in dialogue," a dialogue "into which we can only enter if we make ourselves vulnerable in openness, and if we come away from the dialogue changed."[25]

It would be a mistake, however, to see Moltmann's position as relativistic. Although he relativizes the church and Christianity, he does so precisely because of his conviction that "Christ has come and was sacrificed for the reconciliation of the whole world. No one is excluded."[26] That means that acknowledgement of this event is not necessary to inclusion in it. "The more central the cross becomes, the more open the interest in other religions."[27]

Despite the distance Moltmann and other theologians have come in their openness to other religious traditions, the English philosopher of religion, John Hick, remains critical. He welcomes the openness to dialogue and to being changed by it, but he asks how far this change can be allowed to go. Does the Christian enter dialogue with genuine openness to learn whatever is to be learned, or are there reserved areas?

Hick agrees with Knitter that the major obstacle to truly effective dialogue on the part of Christians is the dominant view of Jesus Christ as absolute. For him, unlike Knitter, this leads to a serious critique of any straightforward assertion of incarnation and Trinity. Christians who enter the dialogue wholeheartedly must be prepared to change their views and commitments with respect to Christology as well as on other topics. Christianity can thereby "move emphatically from the confessional to the truth-seeking stance in dialogue."[28]

For Hick what is involved is a "Copernican revolution." Just as the Ptolemaic theory led to more and more ad hoc modifications to adjust to new data, so the traditional absolutist view of Christian faith has led to more and more ad hoc modifications to adjust it to our new understanding of other religious traditions. The results are equally unconvincing. We need a fundamental reconsideration of the meaning of religion based on a global view. This will lead to the recognition "that the different encounters with the transcendent within the different religious traditions may all be encounters with the one infinite reality, though with partially different and overlapping aspects of that reality."[29] Hick recognizes that this is a familiar idea to Hindus and believes it is important for all. It is this idea which is expressed in the title of his recent book, *God Has Many Names.*

Hick emphasizes that the religions which engage in dialogue are not unified and stable traditions but living movements. "We must not think of the religions as monolithic entities each with its own unchanging character. They are complex streams of human life, continuously changing, though in some periods so slowly that the change is barely perceptible and in other periods so fast that recognizable continuity is endangered."[30] For this reason Christians have no need to cling to established ideas or patterns. We are free to participate in the process of change taking place within the movement. Indeed, today we are called to accelerate those changes.

This is a point even more fully developed by Wilfred Cantwell Smith in a series of volumes culminating in *Toward a World Theology.*[31] Smith rejects the term "religion" in part because it suggests the stable structures which Hick denies and leads to the confrontation of thinkers as representatives of opposing traditions rather than their meeting as believers. Indeed he opposes the plural word "faiths" as adopted by the WCC because it has the same results. He argues that faith is an attribute of human beings everywhere, and that the expression of this in relatively stable and widespread forms is secondary to this fact. He shows in detail how the various traditions interact, at times merging and at times dividing, and he prefers to see himself as part of this whole global movement while acknowledging the strands that have particularly formed him. He aims, therefore, not so much at the development of Christian theology in the global context as at the development of a global theology, even though he recognizes that each formulation of a global theology will bear the imprint of those currents through which the author has been shaped.

There is a point of convergence here between Smith and the dominant strand of WCC thinking. For Smith the dialogue should be between believing people who are only incidentally participants in one community or another. It is their personal faith that they are to share, not the official beliefs of the communities in which they live. But in Smith's case the Christians are in just the same situation as all the others. They are not testifying to an absolute event but to their individual experience of faith. Hence the actual implications of Smith's proposal move far away from WCC theory as that has been influenced by Barth.

Both Hick and Smith stand on the boundary of syncretism. Their programs would move in the direction of those "attempts to create a new religion composed of elements from different religions,"[32] opposed at Nairobi, although neither would favor just this wording. Neither is a syncretist in the sense of failing to recognize specific roots and ties in the Christian heritage. But other twentieth-century thinkers go further in the syncretist direction. Many who survey the scene of competing religions believe that the position from which to think religiously is not within any one religious community but from an independent stance. From that stance they can judge which elements of which traditions meet the needs of contemporary people and can undertake to weave them together into a new unity.

This book is a project in Christian theology; hence fully syncretistic proposals lie outside its scope. One example, however, will clarify this syncretistic way "beyond dialogue" and show how close it is to carrying through proposals already before us. Nicholas Yonker, in *God, Man, and the Planetary Age: Preface for a Theistic Humanism*, teaches that thus far human awareness has passed through four major ages: the primitive age, early civilization, the axial age, and modernity. It "is now in the process of initiating a fifth or Planetary Period, which has the possibility of drawing on the insights of the earlier periods."[33] Yonker spells out in some detail those insights which can be drawn from the several traditions arising in the axial age and also from modernity. He offers a symbol, which he calls the "integrator" which shows how these complementary values can be jointly balanced and realized in a new whole. It is indeed a "global theology" he proposes, and although it has obvious and undenied Christian roots, it is presented not as the next step of Christian development but as the "new religion composed of elements from different religions" which was specifically rejected by the WCC at Nairobi.[34] Yonker believes with good reason that his proposed synthesis could prove attractive to liberal spirits in many traditions.

II. A Critical Evaluation

Thus far this chapter has continued the pattern of the first one in limiting itself to accounts of the views of others. But the purpose of this book is only incidentally to review a history which has led to dialogue as a major mode of relation between Christianity and other religious Ways and to describe current discussion of other traditions and of dialogue with them. The primary purpose of the book is to make a contribution to the systematic theological discussion. This section begins the process of developing that systematic position. It does so by making explicit my evaluations of some of the positions that have been discussed thus far and by engaging a few of them in more extended debate.

The World Council of Churches has been right in opposing or relativizing the category of religion as foundational for dialogue. Our reason for dialogue with others is not that we both participate in a common religiosity. Our common humanity, rather, is the necessary and sufficient basis for dialogue. The Council has been right also in affirming the overriding importance of human community as a reason for dialogue with people both of other faiths and of other ideologies. Nevertheless the World Council is wrong in resisting dealing also with religious traditions as such, and with people as representatives of these religious communities. Kenneth Cragg sees that "religions are great 'wholes,' into which the spirits of men are acclimatized and housed or 'homed'; they are complexes of emotion and mystery and community."[35] The reluctance of the dominant thinkers of the WCC to take seriously these wholes inhibits the WCC from retaining the leadership role in inter-religious dialogue. Learning from other wholes and seeking to influence their further development, if not altogether blocked, are at least subordinated to more secular goals.

The contribution of Jürgen Moltmann, who shares many of the Council's concerns, is very helpful. He makes an advance on the Council's statements in that he calls for dialogue with other religions and by implication sees the importance of dealing with people as representatives of these religions. He overcomes the prejudice against religion and religions that stem from Kraemer and Barth without elevating religion into a normative category. And he stresses Christian openness to being changed in the process of dialogue.

The Roman Catholic church has gone beyond the World Council of Churches in its recognition that all religions and even nonreligious movements such as Marxism play a role in the history of salvation. Christians need to dialogue with representatives of these traditions not only about human community and global liberation but also about salvation religiously conceived. Some Catholic theologians, such as Hans Küng, have gone beyond this to recognize that these traditions can be sufficient bearers of salvation even to the end. Hence the Christian mission is to help them carry out their role in the history of salvation rather than to supersede them. I agree with those Catholics who are concerned that even in these formulations Christians still arrogate to themselves the adjudication as to how and where God is working rather than opening themselves to radical change in the encounter with others and listening to their account of what is taking place.

I agree with Paul Tillich and Wolfhart Pannenberg that the kerygmatic theology that has dominated recent Protestantism and elements of official Catholic orthodoxy blocks both from full openness to the evidence. There should be no special pleading by Christians for Christianity based on ideas of revelation or scriptural authority. Christian theology should work with the available evidence and accept public criticism. Tillich's proposal that this entails viewing Christianity phenomenologically alongside the phenomena of other religions, however, impresses me as failing to take history with sufficient seriousness. Pannenberg's fully historical approach is better. This approach shows that religions are all in the process of change throughout history. Those win and survive in the competition which adjust to new situations and assimilate appropriately from others. This is hindered when the proponents of a religion find their norms in the fixed past. Christianity is freed from this hindrance by its focus on the future as the locus of truth and salvation. Accordingly Christianity can and should assimilate the elements of truth in all other traditions.

Nevertheless, I am made uncomfortable by the apparent implication of Pannenberg's argument that when Christianity has subsumed what is valid in all other traditions it can supersede them all. Although I agree with Pannenberg strongly that the orientation to the future is the key to the present Christian relation to other traditions, I am not sure that they are all so committed to a primordial revelation as to be unable to learn this future orientation from Christianity while we are learning equally valuable lessons from them. Pannenberg's basic and most valuable contribution need not entail the abandonment of pluralism.

I join with Paul Knitter, John Hick, and Wilfred Cantwell Smith in their rejection of the deep-seated tendency of Christians to absolutize our tradition in some way. Of all the major figures treated here only Tillich seems to be completely exempt. Some absolutize Christianity in such a way that it appears that Christians have little to gain from dialogue, at least with respect to matters of central Christian importance. Others so absolutize Christianity as to show that Christians can and should enter into dialogue with every expectation of being transformed in the process, but they still reserve some prius from relativity, a prius in terms of which the whole process is viewed. Knitter, Hick, and Smith note that this absolutist principle is typically bound up with Christology, and they call for Christians to enter dialogue with no reserved areas at all.

They do so in a way that has been rather common in relation to the dialogue. All three believe that every religion centers on the one transcendent divine reality, and they call on Christians to relativize the particular ways in which we have experienced this reality so as to be open to hearing how it has been experienced by others. They know that these experiences and the beliefs and practices associated with them have been multifarious in the extreme, but they are prepared to enter dialogue with complete openness to learning whatever others may have to teach out of their different experience of the one reality.

Despite my agreement with the fundamental intention of these critics, which is to free Christians for true openness to all religions, I believe their proposal is misguided. I shall make my own proposal for a Christocentric approach to the dialogue in debate with them. Much of this will be directed to John Hick, who has gone to some lengths to explain his theory of what is common to all religions and what the differences are. His hypothesis is that there is a noumenal "transcendent ground of all existence, including personal existence"[36] or an "uncreated creator of the universe."[37] All religious experience is of this one reality, although different experiences may be of different aspects of this reality. For lack of any neutral term, he calls this God, but he stresses that the use of this familiar term must not lead to attributing distinctively Christian characteristics to this transcendent ground. We must recognize that experiences in which this ground appears as impersonal are to be given equal credence with those in which it appears as personal. And the personal manifestations must also be allowed to take the most diverse forms.

This is a legitimate hypothesis with which to begin the discussion. Indeed, most dialogue to this day probably proceeds on some such assumption, at least from the Christian side. Nevertheless, I believe that it inhibits authentic dialogue in some instances. Specifically, it inhibits the dialogue with Mahayana Buddhism, which is the one to which this book will give most attention.

Hick is aware that Buddhism is often described as atheistic or nontheistic, but he believes that what is rejected by Buddhists is something more specific and limiting than what he intends by the word God. Buddhists, he thinks, are engaged with some aspect of the same noumenal reality experienced by Christians. The difference is in the way they experience it.

Many Buddhists agree that all religions are dealing with the same reality. But few would accept Hick's account of that reality as the "transcendent ground of all existence, including personal existence." Much of their discipline is devoted to overcoming the notion that there is a ground of any kind. They certainly are not willing to describe the reality with which they are concerned as the uncreated creator of the universe.

Hick may back off from these formulations, recognizing that

they are too determined by Western experience. But one wonders how far he can go. He might fall back on the more general point that "God as humanly known is not God *an sich* but God in relation to mankind, thought and experienced in terms of some particular limited tradition of religious awareness and response."[38] He might accept the fact that grounding all existence is the way God is known in some traditions and not others, but he can hardly give up the notion that God *an sich* is distinct from God as known. Yet that idea is as unacceptable to many Buddhists as are those which reflect the doctrine of God as creator—a doctrine that has been important in the West—for it presupposes a dualism between the human subject and God which Buddhists fundamentally reject. If Hick were prepared to mean by "God" the totality of what is, in every sense of "is" and with whatever unity it has in its multifariousness, then certainly all experience, including all that is called religious, would be experience of some aspect of God. But this would be so radical a change as to set aside most of what he has written on the subject.

The Buddhist might propose that what all religions are truly concerned with is Emptiness or the absolutely immanent process of dependent origination. But it is significant that Emptiness is not an object of worship for Buddhists, whereas there can be little doubt that worship is, for Hick, central to his concerns. Indeed, his initial argument against Christian exclusivism appealed to it: "For it is evident, when one witnesses worship within the great world faiths, including Christianity, that the same sort of thing is going on in each, namely the directing of the worshippers' attention upon a (putative) higher and transcendent reality."[39]

Given this situation it is not illuminating to insist that Emptiness and God are two names for the same noumenal reality. Unless something in the character of the experience warrants that judgment, it is arbitrary, and at the present time the evidence counts in favor of a different hypothesis. If one continues to insist that Buddhist Emptiness is God despite Buddhist objections, the problem that arises is similar to that raised by calling Buddhists anonymous Christians. Knitter, Hick, and Smith agree with Küng in rejecting that approach as arrogant. But is it not equally arrogant to insist that our dialogue partners wrongly interpret their own experience and that we understand it better than they? A better hypothesis might be that where worship is felt to be the appropriate response to religious experience—across the boundaries of many religious traditions—something like what Hick calls God is the reality experienced. On the other hand, where meditation directed toward the realization of what one truly is is the appropriate activity, something like what the Buddhists call Emptiness is the reality that is realized.

My main point here, however, is not to offer a better hypothesis as the basis for dialogue but to argue that we do better to enter dialogue with multiple and flexible hypotheses. We need to make clear that our interest in dialogue does not depend on the correctness of any of these hypotheses, that we enter dialogue in hopes of developing new and better hypotheses. Unfortunately, until now, this attitude has not been widespread, and it is not encouraged by Knitter, Hick, and Smith when they emphasize that all religions are modes of experiencing the one transcendent God.

Insistence on a purely transcendent God as the common ground of religion has negative consequences also for Christian self-understanding. Believing that God is common to the religious traditions and that Christ is particular to Christianity, all three theologians hold that Christians will participate in dialogue more openly if we shift from Christocentrism to theocentrism. Since what is thought to be common to the religious Ways is what is more radically transcendent, along with Christology all concern for divine immanence is downplayed. God is spoken of as the Transcendent or the Absolute. Hick is particularly critical of the doctrines of Trinity and incarnation through which Christians historically have checked the tendency to a one-sided transcendence.

In their moves away from Christocentrism both Knitter and Hick identify it with the idea that Jesus is absolute. There are certainly problems with that view. It seems to deny the full humanity of Jesus or at least his fully personal humanity, and from my perspective such a doctrine deserves rejection quite apart from interest in dialogue with others. But Knitter himself well describes another Christology which he then neglects. "The totality of Jesus is the Christ, the cosmo-theandric principle, the universal revealing and saving presence of God; but the totality of the Christ is not Jesus and cannot be contained in and limited to him."[40] This doctrine has strong grounds in the Christian tradition, and it is this Christ that is central to the faith of many Christians. It is the Christ to whom John Paul II's encyclical *Redemptor Humanis* bears witness.

Our critics could reply that this Christ is God, so that this kind of Christocentrism is really theocentrism after all. This is true. For Christian orthodoxy, Christ is God! But there is a profound religious difference between centering our concern on the revealing and saving presence of God in ourselves and in our world and centering our attention on the noumenal Absolute and its conditioned appearances. In the former case we focus attention on what is happening in the world. In the latter, religion calls us away from this world toward another sphere which alone "has absolute reality and value."[41] To sacrifice belief in the incarnation for the sake of dialogue would not only impoverish us but would also take from us our most precious potential gift to the dialogue partner.

But there is no need for such sacrifice in order to enter dialogue. Our critics are correct that for genuine dialogue we must be open to being changed at any point whatever. That means that we must be prepared to change our Christology, but it equally means that we must be prepared to subject our views of divine transcendence to the test. It does not mean that we downplay in advance our most precious beliefs.

The best dialogue occurs when the partners are deeply convinced of many things. Truth is best approached not by the absence of convictions but by submitting strong convictions to the light of criticism. When one is really convinced, one does not fear such criticism or expect, in advance, that criticism will greatly alter the conviction. Knitter, Smith, and Hick seem quite confident that their monotheism will withstand the challenges of dialogue. Christocentric Christians will be equally confident that dialogue will not destroy our Christocentrism.

Strong convictions about either the transcendent God or Christ are not to be confused with a dogmatic attitude. The dogmatic attitude rejects in advance the relevance of criticism or evidence to the beliefs held. That attitude on any point whatever blocks dialogue. It reflects precisely a lack of real conviction and the substitution of an authoritarian system. This is what Knitter, Hick, and Smith really and legitimately oppose. Their criticism of Christocentrism is misplaced.

Our critics are correct if they judge that Christ remains a distinctively Christian object of commitment. The Confucian heaven or principle, the Vedantist Brahman, and the Buddhist Nirvana cannot be assumed to be synonymous with Christ. Even the Muslim Allah and the Jewish Master of the Universe should be conceived in other terms. But does this mean that devotion to Christ inhibits dialogue or interferes with radical truth-seeking? Surely not. How can one better serve the universal revealing and saving presence of God than by submitting all that one believes to radical questioning and opening oneself critically to alien ideas? Is that not exactly what faith in Christ calls for? The Uppsala report is quite literally correct when it states that Christ is present in authentic dialogue.[42] It is the exemption of beliefs about God or about Christ from real involvement in the dialogue that is an expression of lack of faith in Christ.

This understanding of Christ fits well with the true insight of Hick and Smith that Christianity is a constantly changing movement. When Christ is understood primarily as a fixed event in the ever-receding past, then faithfulness to Christ inevitably requires a certain fixity in the present. Changes in long-held ideas about Christ appear dangerous and threatening. To be Christian is to cling to some relation to that past figure or some belief about him. But if faith is directed instead to the living Christ, the divine saving and revealing presence in our own lives which was truly incarnate in Jesus, then faith in Christ is the free and confident participation in that change which is appropriate to our own time and situation. As Pannenberg shows, we are faithful to Christ not by resisting change but by sensitively participating in the change which God is working in the world. Our need is for discernment, so that the change, which is inevitable, will be a saving or healing change and not rigidification and decay. That means we must be open to the work of God within us and among us, which is Christ, and therefore also open to one another.

III. Beyond Dialogue—Where?

The thesis of this book is that the goal is to go beyond dialogue, yet up to this point the discussion has been almost entirely about how to achieve true dialogue. This is appropriate for two reasons. First, the idea of going beyond dialogue means going beyond what is now officially understood as the proper form of Christian participation in dialogue. Section I above showed that many Christians are seeking to go beyond dialogue in this sense. But this is going beyond inadequate dialogue for the sake of authentic dialogue.

Second, authentic dialogue will necessarily carry us beyond itself. That is, authentic dialogue changes its participants in such a way that new developments beyond dialogue must follow. A statement of how Christians enter dialogue and what kind of outcome they might expect from it will clarify this point.

Although dialogue has its place in all human relationships, the most important dialogues will be those with communities which are most impressive in their attainment of understanding, insight, distinctive experience, community life, or character. It is these from which Christians have most to learn, whether they are religious or not and regardless of how different they are from Christianity. It is these also toward which traditional forms of witness are least likely to be effective. And, indeed, conversion of members of these communities, if it involves their abandonment of those virtues which are distinctive to them, is a doubtful gain. If the conversion of all Jews to Christianity meant the obliteration of Judaism, the world would be a poorer place.

Dialogue with representatives of such groups would be first and foremost for our own sake as Christians. We would hope to enrich our lives and purify our faith by learning from them. We would of course also offer what we believed to be true and valuable in our own tradition. It would be important to us to display its importance in such a way as to challenge our dialogue partners to grow.

But this dialogue, if it succeeds, passes quickly beyond dialogue.

It realizes what is sometimes spoken of as the "risk" of dialogue. That risk is that in the process of listening one will be forced to change in a more than superficial way. Christian dialogue theory is ambiguous with respect to its desire to impose that risk on the partner. It denies the intention to convert, and yet witnesses to Christian truth with the intention that it be heard in all its transformative power. Official dialogue theory has thus far had almost nothing to say about the desirability of fundamental change on the part of the Christian participants, although as we have seen, participants in dialogue are moving vigorously to change this situation.

Beyond dialogue, I suggest, lies the aim of mutual transformation. One may, if one wishes, speak of this as simply another stage of dialogue. However, once a Christian has learned something of first importance from the partner, much of the work of internalizing and integrating this new understanding may better be done in solitude or with other Christians rather than in further conversation. Only when some significant progress has been made in this work will it be important to meet again to take up the dialogue at that new place to which the participants have come.

There is an acute question as to whether one can both play a representative role and also allow oneself to be significantly transformed through dialogue. The transformation that happens to the individuals involved may raise keen suspicions among those whom they initially represented. But changes among leaders, if they are truly leaders, can and do at times affect the communities which they lead. Changes in Catholic and Jewish leaders resulting from dialogue can alter Catholic-Jewish relations at many levels over a period of time. If Christian dialogue with Jews alters the formulations of Christology by those Christians who participate, and if this is truly a representative and influential group of Christians, the implicit anti-Judaism of much of our Christological work may be overcome, and in time preaching and Christian education may be affected. This is a legitimate goal for dialogue and for what lies beyond dialogue.

The emphasis thus far is upon the transformation of Christians and, through Christian individuals, of Christianity. To follow the previous example, it is not clear that Christians can offer much to Jews except apologies until Christianity has been freed of its anti-Judaism. Sensitization to the manifold dimensions and depths of anti-Judaism can be gained by Christians through dialogue with Jews, but the transformation of Christian teaching and practice must be the work of Christians beyond dialogue. The Christianity that would emerge from such a transformation could approach Jews in a quite new way. Its witness to Jesus as the Christ might even be convincing! Perhaps Jews could some day be encouraged to reintegrate into their own history the story of Jesus, and perhaps that would prove an event of transforming significance in the inner history of Judaism. But Christians are not in a position to speak thus to Jews until our own transformation has advanced a long way. The Christian purpose in the dialogue with Jews must be to change Christianity.

What is involved in drawing two communities together is not only a matter of adjustment of doctrine. H. Richard Niebuhr rightly pointed out that what is involved includes the transformation of their respective historical memories. Writing in 1941, Niebuhr focused on the divisions within Christianity and how they might be overcome. He said:

> There will be no union of Catholics and Protestants until through the common memory of Jesus Christ the former repent of the sin of Peter and the latter of the sin of Luther, until Protestants acknowledge Thomas Aquinas as one of their fathers, the Inquisition as their own sin and Ignatius Loyola as one of their own Reformers, until Catholics have canonized Luther and Calvin, done repentance for Protestant nationalism, and appropriated Schleiermacher and Barth as their theologians.[43]

Niebuhr would no doubt be astounded at how far, at least from the Catholic side, there has been movement in the direction he pointed, beginning with the second Vatican Council. What once appeared more as an eschatological dream is being concretely realized, and indeed as Niebuhr foresaw, Protestants and Catholics now work together as Christians out of our common history.

Niebuhr did not deal so explicitly with what would be involved in a similar healing of the great divide between Christians and

Jews. Jesus Christ could not be so unqualifiedly the principle of unity here. But we can repent of the way in which, in the study of history in Christian seminaries, the Jewish community largely disappears from view after the Christian community separates from it. We can begin to appropriate the history of Judaism since that time as the remembered history out of which we live as Christians. We can claim its saints and repent of its sins as we claim Christian saints and repent of Christian sins. In time our language about our "Judeo-Christian tradition" can become real and meaningful. We can see Jesus as truly a part of the Jewish tradition instead of the initiator of a new tradition. We can do little of this without dialogue with Jews.

This emphasis on the transformation of Christianity is the first way in which the purpose of authentic dialogue leads beyond dialogue. But the Christian purpose cannot be only the enrichment and purification of Christianity (and even this must be for the sake of the other as well). Dialogue has a missional goal. That Christians hope to make a difference in others through dialogue should not be concealed.

The difference between dialogue and more conventional forms of witness, it is now clear, is that dialogue is associated with making a contribution to religious communities as communities rather than with the conversion of individual members of the community to Christianity. At least on the Catholic side this has now entered to some extent into official policy. The debate has moved to the next stage. It is between those who see the history of salvation as bringing all the religions finally to Christianity and those who see them as enduring to the end with their separate and valid contributions.

This issue is too sharply posed, chiefly because the transformations of Christianity through dialogue have been too little considered. A Christianity that has genuinely encompassed the history of the Jews in its effective memory and a Judaism which has integrated Jesus into its history will not become one, but the present sharp lines of distinction between them will blur. From such a Judaism Christianity will have much more to learn, and from a Christianity which has in this way been re-Judaized, Jews too will have something to learn. The resultant new stage of the dialogue will again reduce the remaining oppositions. This convergence can be interpreted neither as the movement of Judaism into Christianity nor as simply helping Jews to be better Jews as that is usually understood. We who believe in Christ cannot but believe that becoming better Jews will involve Jews with a new appropriation of Jesus, and by whatever name, a deeper faith in what we know as Christ. But none of this can have present meaning, for we in our conscious and unconscious participation in the long history of Christian anti-Judaism have hardly begun the process of our own purgation and transformation. For that we need the help of the Jews.

I have used the example about which there is likely to be most ready agreement among Christians. Most of our churches do not advocate the effort to proselytize among Jews, convinced in some way that this is not appropriate. Paul's theory suggests not that Jews will join the Gentile churches but that in the fullness of time they will acknowledge Christ. Meanwhile we are beginning to recognize the depths of our historic crime against the Jewish people and to repent.

But in this book I wish to treat a more difficult example, that of Mahayana Buddhism. I believe the pattern here should be similar. At present we are not in a position to offer much to thoughtful Buddhists. The reason is different. Anti-Buddhism is not built into our traditions, and our crimes against Buddhists are not comparable to those against Jews. But Buddhists have a depth of insight into the nature of reality which we lack. As long as a Buddhist's becoming Christian entails abandoning that insight, conversion is not a serious possibility, and it is certainly not a desirable goal of the Christian mission. Until we can share that insight and transform our understanding of our own faith through it, we will have little to say that can or should command Buddhist attention. Hence our present need is to learn through dialogue, and then beyond dialogue to rethink our beliefs. But our purpose in all this cannot be only our own edification and improvement. It must be also to help Buddhists.

We may quite properly say that our concern for the Buddhists is that they become better Buddhists. But as in the preceding case, that can easily be misunderstood. We believe that Buddhists lack something of supreme importance when they do not incorporate Jesus Christ into their Buddhism. We believe they will be better Buddhists when they have done so.

To think of the transformation of Christianity by Buddhism must involve, as in the case of Judaism, the incorporation into our effective memories of Buddhist history. That process has begun. Gautama, at least, is a figure of human history revered also by many Christians. But that is just a beginning. The story of the Buddhist saints and the expansion of Buddhism throughout East Asia is not yet a part of the effective historical memory of Christians. And the history of what took place in Palestine remains outside the effective historical memory of Buddhists. If Buddhism and Christianity are to grow together, both must cultivate a global memory. Since both understand themselves as universal religious traditions, this must be at the same time the road to their own inner fulfillment.

But in the Christian approach to Buddhism the incorporation of historical memories does not suffice. Through their history Buddhists have gained an understanding and experience of reality that is deeper than history. Until Christians have come to appreciate and in some measure to share that understanding and experience, the celebration of Buddhist saints will not do much to bridge the gap.

In these reflections we go beyond the antithesis of all religious traditions moving toward Christianity or each making its permanent separate contribution to the history of salvation. A Christianity which has been transformed by the incorporation of the Buddhist insight into the nature of reality will be a very different Christianity from any we now know. A Buddhism that has incorporated Jesus Christ will be a very different Buddhism from any we now know. That will not obliterate the difference between the two traditions, but it will provide a new basis for fresh dialogue and fresh transformation. The lines that now sharply divide us will increasingly blur.

This proposal is more remote to most present Christian thinking than analogous proposals about Judaism or even Islam. It requires much fuller explanation. The remainder of this book is devoted to clarifying and giving content to the first stages of the new unfolding movement beyond dialogue with Mahayana Buddhism.

NOTES

1. Paul Knitter, "Christianity as Religion: True and Absolute? A Roman Catholic Perspective," in *Concilium, 136. What is Religion?: An Inquiry for Christian Theology,* eds. Mircea Eliade and David Tracy (June 1980). I am indebted to Knitter for much of what I have written here on the post-Vatican II Catholic discussion.

2. Donald K. Swearer, *Dialogue: The Key to Understanding Other Religions* (Philadelphia: Westminster Press, 1977), p. 41.

3. Knitter, "Christianity as Religion," p. 16.

4. M. Zago, "Evangelization in the Religious Situation of Asia," *Concilium:* 114, p. 74.

5. H. Maurier, "The Christian Theology of the Non-Christian Religions," *Lumen Vitae* 31 (1976): 59.

6. Ibid., p. 70.

7. Knitter, "Christianity as Religion," p. 18.

8. Ibid.

9. Ibid., p. 19.

10. James K. Mathews, *A Church Truly Catholic* (Nashville: Abingdon, 1969), p. 160, cited in Samartha, ed., *Living Faiths and the Ecumenical Movement,* p. 152.

11. Stephen Charles Neill, *Christian Faith and Other Faiths* (London: Oxford University Press, 1961), p. 18.

12. Stephen Charles Neill, *Salvation Tomorrow* (Nashville: Abingdon, 1976), p. 42.

13. Ibid., p. 136.

14. Leslie Newbigin, "The Basis, Purpose and Manner of Inter-Faith Dialogue," *Scottish Journal of Theology* 30, vol. 3 (1977): 268.

15. Donald Dawe shows how a careful analysis of the doctrine that we are saved only by the name of Jesus can lead to the conclusion that "Christians must be willing to accept the death of their ideologies to enter into the resurrection of new being." *Christian Faith in a Religiously Pluralistic World,* eds. Donald G. Dawe and John B. Carman (Maryknoll, N.Y.: Orbis Books, 1978), p. 32.

16. Paul Tillich, *The Future of Religions,* ed. Jerald C. Brauer (New York: Harper & Row, 1966), pp. 80–81.

17. Ibid., p. 86.
18. Ibid., p. 87.
19. Ibid., p. 90.
20. Wolfhart Pannenberg, *Basic Questions in Theology II*, trans. George Kehm (Philadelphia: Fortress Press, 1971), p. 113.
21. Ibid., p. 115.
22. Jürgen Moltmann, *The Church in the Power of the Spirit*, trans. Margaret Kohl (London: SCM Press, 1977; New York: Harper & Row, 1977), p. 154.
23. Ibid., pp. 154–55.
24. Ibid., p. 152.
25. Ibid.
26. Ibid., p. 153.
27. Ibid., p. 382, Footnote 42.
28. John Hick, *God Has Many Names: Britain's New Religious Pluralism* (London: Macmillan, 1980), p. 89.
29. John Hick, *God and the Universe of Faiths: Essay in the Philosophy of Religion* (London: Macmillan, 1973), p. 139.
30. Hick, *God Has Many Names*, p. 75.
31. Wilfred Cantwell Smith, *Toward a World Theology* (Philadelphia: Westminster Press, 1981).
32. Carl F. Hallencreutz, *Dialogue and Community*, p. 100.
33. Nicholas Yonker, *God, Man and the Planetary Age: Preface for a Theistic Humanism* (Corvallis: Oregon State University Press, 1978), p. 129.
34. See note 32 above. See Yonker, pp. vii, 108, and 134.
35. Kenneth Cragg, *Preparatory Essays for the Lambeth Conference 1968* (London, 1968), p. 38, cited in Hallencreutz, *Dialogue and Community*, p. 80.
36. John Hick, "Toward a Philosophy of Religious Pluralism," *Neue Zeitschrift für systematische Theologie*, vol. 22, no. 2 (1980): 145.
37. Ibid., p. 142.
38. Ibid., p. 143.
39. Ibid., p. 132.
40. Knitter, "Christianity as Religion," p. 18.
41. Hick, "Towards a Philosophy of Religious Pluralism," p. 147.
42. Hallencreutz, *Dialogue and Community*, p. 77.
43. H. Richard Niebuhr, *The Meaning of Revelation* (New York: Macmillan, 1955), p. 119.

CHAPTER THREE

Western Interpretations of Nirvana

CHAPTER TWO CONCLUDED WITH THE ASSERTION that Buddhism has a peculiarly profound apprehension of reality lacking in our Western Christian heritage. Buddhists apprehend the true reality as Nirvana or Emptiness. The Buddhist goal of attaining Nirvana has fascinated and disturbed Westerners and Christians as long as we have been aware of it. To go through dialogue and beyond with Buddhists must entail our learning from them something of what they mean by Nirvana. The present chapter and the next are devoted to this project. This chapter surveys the story of Western approaches to the understanding of Nirvana. The next offers such systematic understanding as I have attained through study and dialogue.

This chapter is divided into three sections. The first surveys the history of efforts to understand Nirvana from the thirteenth century down to recent times. The efforts summarized in this section all attempted to understand Nirvana in terms of categories available in ordinary Western experience. The second section considers the more successful, but still halting, approach through philosophy. Section III deals with the efforts to understand Nirvana through Christian religious experience.

I. The Scholarly Quest

It is our typical, and I think admirable, Western way that as we confront a major opportunity and challenge we review the history of how we have been dealing with that challenge in the past. The East has not suddenly appeared to us in the 1960s and 1970s. Our ancestors have been fascinated by the East for hundreds, even thousands, of years. I will pick up the story of Western understanding of the East during the European Middle Ages. Beginning in the nineteenth century, I will present in somewhat more detail the efforts of Western scholars to understand the Buddhist doctrine of Nirvana.

Through Friar William of Rubruck and Marco Polo in the thirteenth century and through Jesuit missionaries in the seventeenth and eighteenth centuries, the West received a positive picture of China. Confucian culture was, of all forms of Eastern culture, the most accessible to Westerners. It focused upon personal morality and the social and political order—and China's achievement of order over a vast area was superior to anything attained in Christendom. Further, far from being brutally autocratic and dehumanizing, the Chinese society encountered by these Westerners included elements of humanistic theory and practice that impressed the avant-garde in Europe. The Chinese taught that government existed for the sake of the people, and that the country should accordingly be ruled by those best qualified by virtue and wisdom rather than by those who were born to rank and status. These theories had definite effects upon the institutions of government. The mandarin class was based on examinations open to all, including the humblest peasant, who had the intelligence and discipline to prepare for them.

Both the thirteenth-century writers and the later Jesuits were aware of Buddhists as well, but they did not take Buddhism as seriously. It was for most of them simply a form of idolatry, although some reporters recognized a higher, "atheistic," form. Whereas the Confucian rites and ceremonies were largely political and moral, and the Jesuits at one point persuaded the pope to accept them as such, Buddhist practices seemed antithetical to Christian teaching and did not appear as a challenge to understanding. Even where there were glimpses into the depths of Buddhist experience, the European response was one of horror rather than attraction.

Still the picture was not entirely negative. Christian missionaries were often impressed by Buddhist monastic life and discipline. During the great epoch of Catholic missions to Japan, Buddhist monks, especially of the Zen school, earned the respect of individual Jesuits for their intelligence and devotion, and there were some efforts at theological understanding. But the Christians were baffled by the Buddhist rejection of God and insistence on Nothingness. In any case, the period of dialogue with Japanese Buddhism was brief and left little positive residue.

During the eighteenth century, European admiration of Confucian China began to decline. The Jesuits had reported to Europe the best they could find in China. This had led them to study the Confucian classics and to differentiate pure Confucianism from the neo-Confucianism dominant in China at that time. In their appreciative reports they did not give a full account of the degree of despotism and immorality actually characteristic of Chinese society. As the negative aspects became known in Europe, the Jesuits were discredited and interest in Confucianism declined. Throughout the Enlightenment, Buddhism continued to be viewed as perverse because of its supposed atheism, apathy, and nihilism.

In the nineteenth century, European interest shifted from China to India. This reflects the inner history of European thought as well as the historical contacts with India introduced by British rule there.

The European Enlightenment had been characterized by rationalistic humanism. Its leading thinkers wanted to free society from superstition and supernaturalism and to subject all questions to reason. They believed that when they had done so, humane and progressive institutions would emerge. Confucius appeared to be just the sort of teacher they admired. He did not speculate about metaphysical or theological mysteries but attended to the rational and righteous ordering of human affairs. He respected human beings and saw in them the potentiality for refinement into a healthy culture. He was humane and urbane, following an ethical middle way between rigorism and laxity.

Beginning in the late eighteenth century the romantic movement developed sensitivity to psychic depths and personal needs that were addressed more in India than in Confucian China. As ancient Hindu and Buddhist texts became available, Westerners were fascinated by the likenesses to, and differences from, their own traditions. Buddhism appeared chiefly as a strand of Hindu thought rather than as a separate religious tradition, but it had special appeal, particularly in Great Britain.

The mood in Britain in the nineteenth century was one of nostalgia for a Christian faith that now seemed hard to believe. Jesus remained a powerfully attractive figure, and there was appreciation for the positive achievements of later Christian reformers. The ethics of Christianity were admired and, in large part, subscribed to. But the scientific world view required, in the interpretation of events, abandonment of all such supernatural elements as creation out of nothing, miracles, and the idea of salvation by grace. Any sort of belief in God became problematic. In Buddha the British found a figure equally attractive with Jesus—one who had effected a reformation in India, purifying Indian practice of superstition and idolatry, and Indian thought of speculation. Buddha's ethical teachings were exalted. He taught a religion of self-salvation rather than grace. His world view excluded creation out of nothing and miracles and emphasized *dharma*, which could be understood in Britain as moral and natural law. For Buddha the question of God simply did not arise, and like the evolutionists he assumed a continuity between human beings and the rest of nature which Christians often opposed. In short, he seemed to provide a model religion that fitted the intellectual and moral needs of the time in a way that Christianity did not.

Thus the appeal of Buddhism lay in its embodiment, real or supposed, of those features of Western, and especially Protestant, tradition that were still attractive to sophisticated people in the latter half of the nineteenth century.

But Buddhism was not simply identical with noble personal morality based on an agnostic, scientific world view. It taught release from the world of suffering and it associated this release with the puzzling notion of Nirvana. Here the Western mind seemed to meet in Buddhism something quite alien and hence unacceptable, if not unintelligible. The earlier response of Christian missionaries in Japan and China had been shock at the atheistic character of Nirvana. Agnostic Europeans of the nineteenth century were pleased with the atheism, but they were shocked by Buddhism's apparent negation of human personality and even of life itself. A deeper and more realistic appreciation of Buddhism awaited shifts in Western culture that could render the Buddhist ideal relevant. It also awaited clarification of the meaning of Nirvana. This required a development in Western Buddhist scholarship.

A major role in the establishment of the scholarly study of Buddhism in Europe was played by Eugene Burnouf. Burnouf recognized (in 1844) the central importance for Buddhism of the concept of Nirvana.[1] "Nirvana" names what the Buddhist understands by salvation or deliverance. It entails the extinction or annihilation of individual existence, but the question remains as to what this means. Here two possibilities appear to the Western mind, and Burnouf believed that both were developed in Buddhist schools. One possibility is that Nirvana is absorption into deity; the other, that it is absorption into nothing. The weight of Burnouf's scholarship led to the view that Buddhism was atheistic and that, accordingly, Nirvana is sheer extinction.

Much of European reflection about Buddhism was shaped by these conclusions of Burnouf's. John Stuart Mill held that the widespread appeal of Buddhism showed that ordinary people can accept annihilation as their destiny with equanimity. But the general view was decidedly otherwise. It was incredible to most nineteenth-century Europeans that extinction or annihilation could be regarded by any sane person as a goal to be arduously sought.

Max Müller was Burnouf's most important student and the leading Indologist of the second half of the nineteenth century. As such, although he directed most of his attention to Hindu studies, he carried great weight also in his views on Buddhism. Müller believed that the basic content of all religion is the "perception of the infinite."[2] He was further convinced that human beings universally yearn for life and finally for immortality. Hence he found it incredible that hundreds of millions of people could have adopted a religion devoted to annihilation. He wrote that "to believe . . . that one half of mankind had yearned for total annihilation would be tantamount to belief that there is a difference in kind between man and man."[3] That human beings could differ from one another in their essential nature was unthinkable. Hence Nirvana must, Müller insisted, be something like Christian immortality.

But Müller recognized that Nirvana in its root meaning does mean extinction or annihilation. He was too good a scholar to attempt to evade this fact. Further, he found that in much of Buddhist literature this negative note was pursued vigorously and unflinchingly. Hence he confronted a dilemma: Buddhism's teaching in its most fully articulated form could not but deeply repel all sane human beings, yet it had won its way over half the world!

Müller could not resolve this conflict between his own deepest convictions about human nature and his scholarly recognition of historical facts, but he did manage to come to terms with it in his own way. The nihilistic texts, he showed, were the most theoretical or philosophical ones, and hence the ones most remote from the roots of religious life. The meaning of Nirvana that has religious appeal is "the entrance of the soul into rest, a subduing of all wishes and desires, indifference to joy and pain, to good and evil, and absorption of the soul in itself and a freedom from the circle of existence from birth to death, and from death to a new birth."[4]

Others understood Nirvana as a state of existence that could be adequately described without reference to any kind of infinity or deity. For them Nirvana was a form of this-worldly experience. As early as 1700, Christian missionaries had described Nirvana in terms of Stoic apathy. In 1827, Henry Thomas Colebrooke wrote that Nirvana is "a condition of unmixed tranquil happiness or ecstasy . . . a happy state of imperturbable apathy."[5] But the idealization of apathy was as objectionable to Europeans as was the goal of extinction. It was only when Rhys Davids provided a new description of this state of blessedness that Nirvana could finally be rendered attractive to the dominant nineteenth-century European mind. He argued that "the Nirvana taught by early Buddhists was a moral condition, a modification of character, to be brought about by personal self-control and self-discipline of mind and heart; a state of peace, goodness, and wisdom, attainable here, in this life, and in this world."[6]

However, Rhys Davids's view failed to withstand critical questioning, and in the first third of the twentieth century the alternatives were reduced again to two. LaVallée Poussin, after a lifetime of Buddhist scholarship, reached conclusions close to those reached earlier by Max Müller. He distinguished the original and primary understanding of Nirvana from the philosophical formulations. These latter, Poussin agreed, develop the logic of certain basic ideas in a way that leads to the identification of Nirvana with annihilation. But the primary meaning was deliverance from the sphere of suffering and mortality, and Nirvana named the sphere of immortality into which this deliverance brings the saint. Deliverance is achieved by a particular discipline and yoga, "without definite speculative tendencies and without exclusive or particular devotional practices."[7]

This belittling of the negative meaning of Nirvana was completely unacceptable to the other great Buddhologist of the period, Theodor Stcherbatsky. Stcherbatsky was convinced that the discovery of an original Buddhism, free from doctrine, behind the theoretical elaborations of our actual sources, expressed the desires of modern scholars rather than historical probabilities. For him the later speculative elaborations accurately witness to basic features of original Buddhism in whose service they are developed. Thus the philosophical arguments justifying the denial of substantial entities or persons witness to the centrality of these denials in normative Buddhism.

Nevertheless, Stcherbatsky's closer attention to the philosophical schools shows that their arguments do not lend to annihilation *simpliciter.* He sees three periods of Buddhist thought in India.

> Each of them has its central conception; they are respectively Pluralism, Monism, and Idealism. The Sanskrit terms designating them are *pudgala-sunyata*, *sarva-dharma-sunyata*, and *bahya-artha-sunyata*. These are negative definitions meaning: (1) Unreality of the Ego, (2) Unreality of all the Elements of Existence, (3) Unreality of the External World. Their implied positive meaning is respectively, (1) Plurality of interrelated and ultimate Elements of the Personality, (2) Relativity and consequent Unreality of all these Elements, and the unique Reality of the Immutable Whole, (3) Ideality of these Elements and of all cognizable things. Disregarding the pluralism, relativity, and ideality of the elements of exis-

> tence, there are these elements themselves, the "elementariness" of Existence, the denial of a permanent substantial Ego, and the splitting of it into separate elements—that is the central conception out of which all the subsequent diversity of doctrine developed.[8]

The quest for the meaning of Nirvana from Burnouf to Stcherbatsky reminds one of the quest for the historical Jesus, which was occurring during much of the same period. Although the quests were stimulated at times by those who were antagonistic to Nirvana on the one hand and to Jesus on the other, most participants were motivated by the desire to make their subjects intelligible and attractive. Accordingly, Nirvana, like Jesus, was assimilated as far as possible to categories of understanding acceptable in cultured European circles of the time. Yet in both cases the integrity of the scholarship inhibited the assimilation and forced the recognition that there was something profoundly alien in the subject matter. Just as Jesus did not fulfill the ideals of Romantics or Victorians, so also Nirvana did not represent their goals. But in both cases what was initially denied, or rejected as alien, was to come in the course of time to have a positive attraction.

This survey also reminds us of a limitation of scholarship that we sometimes forget. The texts will yield answers only to the questions that are asked of them. If the texts themselves speak of other matters related to other questions, their meaning eludes the scholar. European scholars assumed that Nirvana must refer either to salvation in this life or to salvation after death. If the former, then it must be describable in moral and psychological terms. If the latter, then it must be union with God or simply extinction.

The debate went on and on, and remained unresolved, for the crucial texts actually spoke neither of moral and psychological change nor of absorption into God or nothingness. They spoke instead of actual experience in this life, but in terms of much more radical change than the Western interpreters could envision—an alteration of the very structure of human existence. They spoke of the extinction of the self as a fundamental reversal of all ordinary reality, a radical transformation of experience. The doctrine that this might be perfected at death did not introduce the Western difference between this-worldly and otherworldly salvation. In short, the categories of thought with which Western Buddhologists approached their texts did not allow the texts to be understood.

II. The Philosophical Approach

Whereas scholars as scholars normally employ the language and conceptuality that is provided for them, philosophers need not do so. Indeed, in the great tradition of philosophy the major figures have each provided a new way of envisioning reality. If Nirvana did not fit any of the categories provided in ordinary Western language, there remained the possibility that it could be understood philosophically.

The first philosopher to attempt this was Arthur Schopenhauer (1788–1860). He wrote when Buddhist scholarship was young, and he knew the Buddhist texts only in unreliable translations. But he was deeply revolted by the attachment of ordinary people and philosophers alike to the world of common sense, and his own intellectual and spiritual struggle against this attachment prepared him to understand Buddhism with an impressive profundity.

Schopenhauer believed that the phenomenal world is a product of the human will, that this world is fundamentally characterized by suffering, and that salvation can consist only in the extinction of the will. This extinction is so basic a change that we can form no notion of what experience is like when it has occurred. We can only glimpse the results in the lives of saints and mystics. Schopenhauer held that this radical reversal of what we falsely experience as reality is the essential message of Christianity, but he saw this message as profoundly obscured by Christianity's theism, its ideas of creation and of the goodness of the world, its anthropocentrism, and its moralism. He discovered the message more purely and clearly expressed in Buddhism. Nirvana, he recognized, is that totally unimaginable, blessed condition realized when one's will, and with it all that we know as reality, is extinguished.

Obviously Schopenhauer's view cannot pass muster as an exact, scholarly account of Nirvana. His Kantian distinction of noumena and phenomena, and his stress on the will in distinction from the Buddhist talk of craving, place him in a different philosophical context. But his passion for a salvation that involves the abolition of ordinary reality by the annihilation of the personal center is astoundingly similar to Buddhism, and his insight into the meaning of Nirvana was correspondingly acute. It is unfortunate that Western scholars of Buddhism continued to operate with dominant Western categories and hence neglected the intuitions of Schopenhauer.

Martin Heidegger, a century later, came to a vision corresponding to that of Buddhism through a quite different channel. He began his philosophical work seeking to uncover the understanding of being *(Sein)* which has been obscured by the Western interest in beings *(die Seienden)*, their analysis, and their manipulation. He thought that the way to grasp being would be through the analysis of that being who asks the question of being, namely, the human being. With this aim he wrote his extremely influential book, *Being and Time*, a phenomenological account of *Dasein* or human existence. However, he found that being eluded him still.

Heidegger thereupon shifted his approach. Whereas in *Being and Time* he depicted *Dasein* as authentic when it took responsibility for its own projects, in his later writings he gave the primacy to being as such. He denied that this being was the Being of traditional Western metaphysics, which he said was based on the "ontotheological" understanding of being. And certainly being is not *a* being. The ontological difference between being and beings is crucial.

Since being cannot be stated or described in language, language must allow itself to be shaped by being. In this way being is not conceptualized, but it is able to speak. Heidegger's later writings are intended to evoke our awareness of being rather than to speak of being. The goal is more the realization of being in us than the intellectual comprehension of being.

None of this was developed with Buddhism in view. But whereas the traditional understanding of Being Itself had affinities with the Hindu Brahman, Heidegger's completely nonsubstantial and nondual being has remarkable affinities with Nirvana or Emptiness. This was recognized by many Oriental scholars and led to an exchange with a Zen practitioner. Thus again a philosophical reconceptualization in the West built a bridge to the understanding of Buddhism.

There is a high price to pay, however, for using the bridges offered by Schopenhauer or Heidegger. If one passes over on these bridges there is no way to come back. That is, if one accepts Schopenhauer's or Heidegger's analysis, one may be able to enter into the world of Buddhist experience, but one is shut off from the Christian world. Buddhism can be understood only by rejecting Western modes of thought and experience.

A third philosopher will detain us longer, not because he is more profound, but because he offers us the possibility of thinking of both the Eastern and the Western modes of experience as valid. This is F. S. C. Northrop, whose *The Meeting of East and West* was first published in 1946 as a pioneering argument that the basic visions of East and West are complementary. Both necessarily begin in the sheer immediacy of experience, which Northrop calls the differentiated aesthetic continuum. But the West juxtaposes to this immediacy an "unseen theoretic component which can be adequately designated only by thought and postulationally prescribed theory checked through its deductive consequences."[9] That is, the West has developed logical, ontological, theological, mathematical, and scientific ideas, which it correlates with the immediate data of the senses. These range from the existence of a transcendent God as creator of all things to the theory of gravitational attraction between material particles. None of this has interested the East, which has moved instead through the differentiated aesthetic continuum to its undifferentiated ground.

This condensed statement requires unpacking. We all begin in our immediate experience. That experience already includes concepts and ideas such as "tables" and "walls" and "dogs" and "people." But it does not take much reflection to see that these concepts are not part of the most primary experience. They orient us in our world, but this orientation is only one among several possible orientations. If we had grown up in another culture, we would have been oriented differently. Each language involves its own way of orienting those who use it. We also learn, through the study of history and philosophy and art, that some individuals have been able to experience the world in ways that differ from the cultural habits of their time and then to teach others to adopt their new ways.

In the West, Northrop teaches, we have concentrated attention on our organized experience, an experience already permeated by our ideas. In the East there has been more awareness that ideas distort as much as they illumine—perhaps more. Hence the East has attended more than the West to the primary experience that is not yet shaped by ideas or concepts. It is this preconceptualized experience that Northrop calls the differentiated aesthetic continuum. Instead of seeking the best conceptuality available, as the West has done, the East stays close to this continuum, experiencing it as a flux of sensa. Like the West, the East goes beyond this flux, but whereas the West transcends it through ideas, the East probes beyond it in a different direction. It encourages disciplines that develop the recognition that the elements which distinguish one experience from another—the particular colors and sounds that make up each experience—are not ultimate. Hence the East points to a deeper and more fundamental reality, which Northrop identifies as the *un*differentiated aesthetic continuum, that is, as what is left when the sense data are removed from the continuum of immediate experience. This is something like pure extensiveness apart from anything extended.

The distinction Northrop makes is an important one, and it is illuminating of the West. On the other hand, it exaggerates the role of the differentiated aesthetic continuum as the starting point of Eastern thought. The next chapter will describe one form of Eastern experience in more detail and somewhat differently. But in this respect Northrop's error is a subtle one.

A more obvious weakness of Northrop's theory is that it does not do justice to the variety of Eastern cultures. His book deals profoundly with the variety of Western cultures, but it treats India and China as expressions of a common basic orientation. The tendency of more recent typologies is quite different. When viewed globally there appear to be three major forms of cultural and religious life: Indian, Chinese, and Western. E. A. Burtt presents India as most interested in the self and its growth toward cosmic maturity, China as preoccupied with society and harmonious interpersonal relations, and the West as absorbed with individualism, analysis, and the external world.[10] Yves Congar describes India as idealistic, China as naturalistic, and the West as dualistic.[11] Huston Smith asserts that "the West has accented the natural problem, China the social, and India the psychological."[12] John Hutchison describes the dominant religions of India, China, and the West respectively as acosmic, cosmic, and theistic.[13]

There is thus a wide consensus that the cultures of India and China are quite distinct, and it is doubtful that Northrop's account of the East fits either accurately. Clearly, therefore, his theory requires revision. But in two respects it remains a model which has been rarely equaled. First, it presses the analysis of the differences to their experiential roots, and second, it enables us to see how East and West can be mutually complementary.

To assert that East and West are complementary is to make a very important statement. If it is correct, then we might be able to realize the ideal of a global culture that synthesizes the greatest achievements of our diverse civilizations. At least the encounter of East and West should offer the possibility to each of enrichment by the other without loss of its own soul.

Northrop's doctrine of complementarity is a rejection of two more common views. It rejects, first, the view that human experience is everywhere basically alike, that differences are superficial, and that accordingly the task for Westerners is to interpret the East in terms of familiar Western experience. It rejects, second, the view that the differences between East and West amount to contradictions. If the Eastern and Western views were contradictory, then to accept the Eastern view of nature, humanity, or divinity would be to reject what is essential to the Western view. My thesis, following Northrop, is that although what we find in the East is profoundly different from what we have achieved in the West, there is no contradiction. *In principle* what we learn from the East can complement our achievement. I say, "in principle," for on the surface East and West appear to contradict each other in point after point. Only through deeper analysis can apparent contradictions be converted into mutually enriching contrasts.

III. The Religious Approach

In the twentieth century there has been increasing recognition on the part of Westerners that the understanding of Eastern thought in general and Buddhism in particular requires what John Dunne has taught us to call "passing over."[14] This is a matter of using all the clues we can to gain an imaginative identification with the other so that we can try to understand from the inside. This opens up the possibility of expanding the repertoire of categories in terms of which a strange phenomenon may be grasped. After one has passed over one must come back to one's own world with the extension of imaginative experience.

Jacques-Albert Cuttat writes:

> A fanatic is not one who considers that some particular tenet of Eastern religions is incompatible with the Christian dogma, an obvious fact on the level of human formulations; instead, a fanatic is a person unwilling to ask himself what really takes place between God and the soul of the Oriental who, after the most disinterested ascetic efforts, reaches what he calls *nirvâna, samâdhi* or *tawhîd.*[15]

This is a call for passing over. Its danger is that because the terms of the imagination are set by Western categories it will not go far enough toward understanding the Nirvana experience in its uniqueness.

The classic work on the understanding of Eastern religion through the examination of religious experience is Rudolf Otto's *Mysticism East and West.*[16] Otto showed remarkable similarities between some forms of Christian and Hindu mysticism, especially those of Meister Eckhart and Sankara. Westerners acquainted with their own mystical tradition were given a fresh access to important forms of Hindu religion. This has encouraged efforts to use the same tradition as a bridge to the understanding of Buddhism. In this approach Nirvana too is understood as fundamentally identical with the Godhead with whom Eckhart sought union. Buddhists attracted to Eckhart have at times encouraged this understanding.

Increasingly, Vedantist mysticism was recognized as the most fully developed form. Other religious traditions, Eastern and Western, were searched for expressions of the same fundamental experience. Aldous Huxley, in *The Perennial Philosophy,*[17] assembled and interpreted mystical sayings from all the major traditions. In this context Buddhism appears as a variant expression of the mystical experience of its Hindu parent. Nirvana is seen as a different name for that one ultimate reality called elsewhere Allah, Godhead, Tao, or Brahman.

This tradition of Western scholarship gains fresh expression in Frithjof Schuon's *The Transcendent Unity of Religion.*[18] Schuon distinguishes an esoteric and an exoteric element in all religions, holding that the esoteric experience of universal identity or deity is the common ground from which the exoteric diversities arise.

In this century and especially since World War II a new factor has been present in the Western interpretation of Buddhism. This is the practicality of dialogue between the best representatives of East and West. Study of ancient texts is now supplemented by encounter with living Buddhists who are fully capable of sharing in exacting textual study, discussing with Western scholars on their own terms, and at the same time speaking out of the experience to which the texts point. These Buddhists are chiefly, but not exclusively, Japanese who stand in the Zen tradition and have been inspired by the philosopher Kitaro Nishida, who died in 1945. Dialogue with such representatives combined with the possibility of practicing Buddhist meditation, opens a new chapter in the West's understanding of Buddhism.

The most influential figure in this dialogue from the Buddhist side has been D. T. Suzuki, who devoted much of his life to interpreting Zen Buddhism to Westerners. Meanwhile on the American scene, Catholic mysticism took on new life and visibility through Thomas Merton. In 1961 a dialogue between these two men was published in *New Directions 17.* In this dialogue Suzuki describes Christianity as "affective, personal, and dualistic," whereas Zen is "nonaffective, nonpersonal, and nondualistic."[19] Merton agrees that "the strongly personalistic tone of Christian mysticism, even when it is 'apophatic,' generally seems to prohibit a full equation with Zen experience"[20] but he formulates the distinction differently. "For the Buddhist, life is a static and ontological fullness. For the Christian it is a dynamic gift, a fullness of love."[21]

The key term for Zen is Emptiness *(Sunyata)* which is equivalent to Nirvana. Suzuki finds a point of contact for explaining Zen Emptiness in the Christian concept of poverty. Merton associates Emptiness also with the Christian goal of purity of heart. But he holds that purity of heart is not the ultimate end. It is the ground of a fresh start.[22] "Purity of heart establishes man in a state of unity and emptiness in which he is one with God. But this is the necessary preparation . . . for the real work of God which is revealed in the Bible: the work of the *new creation*, the resurrection from the dead, the restoration of all things in Christ."[23] Thus for Merton the Buddhist goal, Emptiness or Nirvana, is equivalent to an experience attained by the Christian as a way station toward the kingdom of God.

Suzuki believed that this relegation of Zen to the first stage of the Christian experience betrayed that Merton's Emptiness "does not go far and deep enough."[24] It relates the Christian to God but not to the Godhead. Zen Emptiness does not open one to being filled by God but is itself the fullness of the Godhead.

Despite this criticism, Suzuki gives encouragement to Christians interested in the practice of Zen. He asserts that Zen may be practiced by "a Taoist, a Confucian, even a Shintoist," and that "Zen experience can also be explained by Western philosophy."[25] Or again, Zen "is extremely flexible in adapting itself to almost any philosophy and moral doctrine as long as its intuitive teaching is not interfered with."[26] Merton reasonably concludes that Zen is not bound to any structure, even that of Buddhism.[27] At the same time it is the purest form of Buddhism, since Buddhism aims at just this freedom from structure. Hence Merton set out "to become as good a Buddhist" as he could.[28] He came to see Zen as the best means of attaining the first stage of Christian mystical experience.[29]

Clearly the dialogue of a Western mystic with an Eastern Zenist has led to an appreciative understanding very different from anything that appeared earlier. Zen can now be viewed as a superior means of achieving important, though limited, Christian goals. Although the published dialogue leaves many questions, and although Merton's untimely death denied us the full fruits of his continuing and disciplined passing over into Buddhism, he inspired the continuation of dialogue between Zen leaders and Christian mystics in Japan. William Johnston is now the key figure in that dialogue.

In 1970 Johnston published *The Still Point: Reflections on Zen and Christian Mysticism.* He is clear that in Zen there is an experience not to be found in the Christian tradition. "In Christian mysticism, in Zen, in the aesthetic experiences of T. S. Eliot, we are touching a realm of the psychic life which has many divisions and compartments and sections. I mean the whole field of supraconceptuality is extremely varied."[30] Thus there are many types of experience which leave the subject-object distinction behind.[31] Zen is only one. Nevertheless, Johnston guides toward an understanding of Nirvana or *satori* by numerous comparisons with Western mystical experience and yoga. "The special characteristic of Zen . . . is the *muga:* the ego is lost—not lost in the type of Yoga concentration in which consciousness, drained of all content whatsoever, remains 'pure' or blank without an ego; but rather lost because of the identification of subject and object."[32]

Johnston has no doubt about the value of this experience both for physical and emotional health and also for spirituality. "I would suggest . . . that the Zen techniques can teach the Christian how to relax, how to be calm, how to think in a deeper way, how to dispose himself to receive God's love, how to conceive the truths of faith not only in his brain but in his whole body."[33] Nevertheless Johnston recognizes that when a Christian uses Zen the experience is not the same as for a Buddhist. "Christians and Buddhists agree that meditation is not totally divorced from one's philosophy of life."[34]

Approaching Buddhism through religious experience does not necessarily employ mystical experience as the point of contact, although when it focuses elsewhere, it does not lead so directly toward an understanding of Nirvana. The Christian understanding of the cross and resurrection as the dying to the old self and the rising to the new can be employed as a point of contact for understanding the no-self doctrine of Buddhism. When the Buddhist doctrine has been understood, according to Donald Swearer, the Christian "may rediscover the deepest meaning of the spiritual journey from the Old to the New Creation. Furthermore, he will come to see the life of Christ as one where the old self-image has been crucified so that a new being in the likeness of God might emerge."[35] This is a particularly good example of that passing over and coming back through which a true understanding of Buddhism can be attained.[36]

Donald Swearer writes out of extensive experience of Theravada Buddhism in Thailand. Winston King earlier wrote a substantial comparison of Buddhism and Christianity based on a twenty-month stay in Burma.[37] Frederick J. Streng has written a brilliant study, *Emptiness: A Study in Religious Meaning*,[38] reflecting a deep passing over into the material. These books represent a new generation that combines the methods of the scholarly study of the history of religions with an imaginative and existential involvement in dialogue. A responsible understanding of Buddhism in general and of Nirvana in particular has now become possible.

NOTES

1. Guy Richard Welbon, *The Buddhist Nirvana and its Western Interpreters* (Chicago: The University of Chicago Press, 1968), p. 58.
2. Max Müller, *Lectures on the Origin and Growth of Religion* (London: Longman's, Green, and Co., 1880), pp. 26–27, cited in Welbon, *Buddhist Nirvana*, p. 108.
3. Max Müller, *Selected Essays on Language, Mythology, and Religion, II* (London: Longman's, Green, and Co., 1881), pp. 220–21, cited in Welbon, *Buddhist Nirvana*, p. 118.
4. Müller, *Selected Essays, II*, pp. 305–6, cited in Welbon, *Buddhist Nirvana*, p. 125.
5. Henry Thomas Colebrooke, *Miscellaneous Essays, II*, ed. E. B. Colwell (London: Trübner and Co., 1873), p. 425, cited in Welbon, *Buddhist Nirvana*, p. 28.

6. Rhys Davids, "The Buddhist Doctrine of Nirvana," *Contemporary Review* 29 (1877): 267, cited in Christopher Clausen, "Victorian Buddhism and the Origins of Comparative Religion," *Religion: Journal of Religion and Religions* 5 (Spring, 1975): 12.

7. LaVallée Poussin, *Nirvana* (Paris: Cabriel Beauchesne, 1925), p. 53, cited in Welbon, *Buddhist Nirvana*, p. 282.

8. Theodor Stcherbatsky, "The Doctrine of the Buddha," *Bulletin of the School of Oriental Studies* 6 (1930–1932): 871, cited in Welbon, *Buddhist Nirvana*, p. 288.

9. Filmer Stuart Cuckow Northrop, *The Meeting of East and West* (New York: Macmillan, 1946), p. 450.

10. E. A. Burtt, "How Can the Philosophies of East and West Meet?" *The Philosophical Review* 57, no. 6 (November 1948).

11. Yves Congar, *Toward the Unification of the Faiths* (Calcutta: Calcutta University Press, 1957).

12. Huston Smith, "Accents of the World's Philosophies," *Philosophy East and West* (April–July 1957): 8.

13. John Hutchison, *Paths of Faith* (New York: McGraw Hill, 1969).

14. John Dunne, *The Way of All The World* (New York: Macmillan, 1972), p. ix.

15. Jacques-Albert Cuttat, *The Encounter of Religions: A Dialogue Between the West and the Orient*, trans. Pierre de Fontnouvelle (New York: Desclee Co., 1960), p. 68.

16. Rudolf Otto, *Mysticism East and West* (New York: Macmillan, 1932).

17. Aldous Huxley, *The Perennial Philosophy* (New York: Harper & Brothers, 1945).

18. Frithjof Schuon, *The Transcendent Unity of Religion*, trans. Peter Townsend (New York: Harper & Row, 1975). French original, 1948.

19. See Thomas Merton, *Zen and the Birds of Appetite* (New York: New Directions, 1968), p. 133.

20. Ibid., p. 135.

21. Ibid., p. 138.

22. Ibid., p. 131.

23. Ibid., p. 132.

24. Ibid., p. 133.

25. Daisetz Teitarō Suzuki, *Zen and Japanese Culture*. Rev. 2nd ed. (New York: Pantheon Books, 1959), quoted in Nancy Wilson Ross, *Three Ways of Asian Wisdom* (New York: Simon & Schuster, 1966), p. 142.

26. Suzuki, *Zen and Japanese Culture*, p. 63.

27. Merton, *Zen and the Birds of Appetite*, p. 4.

28. Raymond Bailey, *Thomas Merton on Mysticism* (Garden City, New York: Doubleday, 1975), p. 174.

29. It is striking that a similar evaluation of Buddhism, this time in

relation to Hindu mysticism, is found in Sri Aurobindo. See Satprem, *Sri Aurobindo, or the Adventure of Consciousness*, trans. Tehmi (New York: India Library Society, 1964), pp. 138–46. On p. 141 a passage is quoted from *Sri Aurobindo on Himself and on the Mother* (1953), p. 154, as follows: "Nirvana in my liberated consciousness turned out to be the beginning of my realisation, a first step towards the complete thing, not the sole true attainment possible or even a culminating finale."

30. William Johnston, *The Still Point: Reflections on Zen and Christian Mysticism* (New York: Fordham University Press, 1970), p. 77.

31. Ibid., p. 51.

32. Ibid., p. 57.

33. Ibid., p. 171.

34. Ibid., p. 175.

35. Donald K. Swearer, *Dialogue: The Key to Understanding Other Religions* (Philadelphia: Westminster Press, 1977), p. 83.

36. See also the report on the conference at Oiso in 1967 sponsored by the Quakers and chaired by Douglas V. Steere in Heinrich Dumoulin, *Christianity Meets Buddhism* (LaSalle, Illinois: Open Court Press, 1974), pp. 42–56.

37. Winston King. *Buddhism and Christianity: Some Bridges of Understanding* (Philadelphia: Westminster Press, 1963).

38. Frederick J. Streng, *Emptiness: A Study in Religious Meaning* (Nashville: Abingdon Press, 1967).

CHAPTER FOUR

Passing Over

CHAPTER THREE SURVEYED THE HISTORY of the failure of scholarly attempts to grasp Nirvana in established Western categories and then showed how progress had been made through combining scholarship with philosophy and religious experience. The task of this chapter will be to present a more or less coherent understanding of Nirvana or Emptiness in its contrast to familiar Western and Christian ideas. Although the account will be quite different from that of F. S. C. Northrop, I am encouraged by him to believe that after passing over to an understanding of Buddhism, it will be possible to come back and to display a complementary relation between Nirvana and the Christian faith. That will be the task of Chapter Five.

The philosophy from which I receive most help in passing over and returning is that of Alfred North Whitehead. Whitehead was the teacher of Northrop, and Northrop's basic categories are derived from Whitehead. But Northrop both simplified Whitehead's conceptuality and failed to develop aspects of it which appear fruitful for a more differentiated account of Eastern views and especially of Buddhism.

It would be absurd to claim that the understanding of Nirvana that here comes to expression is *the* Buddhist understanding. It is, first of all, oriented to Mahayana rather than Theravada. As indicated in the preface, it has been attained chiefly through dialogue with a few Japanese Buddhists, mostly Zen but some from the Pure Land tradition, combined with modest study of some texts in English translation and of secondary literature. Nevertheless, I believe that what I offer is an approximation of the normal and normative understanding of Nirvana.

There are other topics besides Nirvana that belong to an adequate dialogue with Mahayana Buddhist thought. Still it may be that there is a difference between the center of Buddhist wisdom and the periphery. If the dialogue deals chiefly with the periphery much may be learned, but even the peripheral matters will not be truly understood. Points of apparent understanding and agreement will dissolve into perplexity when the periphery is not grasped in relation to the center. Buddhist organization and monasticism, Buddhist views of history and society, Buddhist ethics and psychology, the Buddhist doctrines of *karma*, suffering, guilt, and death, the Buddhist attitude toward scripture, toward nature, or toward art—all these are surely important and interesting subjects for dialogue, and much can be understood about them when they are discussed. But they are not the heart of the matter for Buddhists. The heart of the matter is Nirvana or Emptiness. And until this is understood, there can be no adequate understanding of the other topics either.

For this reason the discussion of Nirvana in this chapter and the next should not be treated as the selection of simply one of the many interesting topics available for dialogue. It is intended as a way of moving to the core issue between Buddhism and Christianity, the essential challenge Buddhism poses to Christians. If Christianity can assimilate the Buddhist insight here, it can deal with the other issues with some confidence.

I will approach the topic in four ways. The first section describes Nirvana as the cessation of all craving or clinging, including attachment to God, to self, and to understanding. In Section II Nirvana is presented as the extinction of the self or, more accurately, as the realization that there has never been a self to extinguish. Section III discusses Nirvana as ultimate reality. It is a profoundly different idea from the biblical idea of God. In their deepest meaning, these two, far from meeting, display a basic contrast. The fourth section deals with the attitude toward time expressed by Nirvana. This is far removed from our biblically formed Western sense of linear time and of the meaning of history.

Since the reality discussed is the same in all four sections, they must inevitably be somewhat repetitive. But Nirvana is the answer to multiple questions. It remains sufficiently difficult for the Westerner to understand that a little redundancy may not be amiss.

I. The Cessation of Clinging

Buddhism begins with the judgment that all life is suffering and proceeds to analyze why that is so and how suffering can be overcome.[1] The heart of the analysis is that we suffer because we are attached to things—we desire or cling to them. When we relinquish this attachment, when we cease to cling, we become free.

Chapter Three noted that Westerners have sometimes seen this in its resemblance to the Stoic analysis. Stoicism teaches that we all seek happiness, but that as long as our happiness depends upon anything that is not within our power as individuals it eludes us. We can be happy only if we limit our desires to those things that we control. That means giving up all concern about what may be done to us physically or the opinion that others have of us. It means abandonment of hopes and fears as to what happens to others as well. If we desire only to be rational, then we can fulfill our desire and no one can interfere. Thereby we attain happiness.

Buddhism does resemble Stoicism to a point. Buddhists, like Stoics, must cease to care what others do to them or think of them. They must also detach themselves from concern for others. Worry about friends and relatives is as destructive as anxiety about what will happen to ourselves.

Nevertheless, the differences are vast. Although Stoicism has always appeared in the West as an extremely radical doctrine, it does not go as far as Buddhism. The Stoic is attached to his or her own rationality or virtue. The Buddhist must be attached to nothing. Further, the Stoic life would not impress the Buddhist as being free from suffering. It appears to be one of strong-willed endurance and self-control, whereas when clinging is abandoned there is perfect freedom.

The similarity may be closer with Christianity. Christians also know that attachment to the world leads to suffering. Maturing in spirit involves overcoming our craving for worldly security, reputation, success, and achievement. This is not easy to accomplish! Some Christians have engaged in harsh ascetic practices, but others have known, like Buddhists, that such practices are as likely to bind as to free. Some Christians have meditated on the ephemeral character of all worldly things as a way to reduce the attractiveness of worldly goods and hence the desire for them. In medieval monasteries the human skull functioned as a symbol of the futility of worldly goals. There are parallel practices to be found in Buddhist meditation.

There are similarities also in practical expressions of freedom from clinging. In both Christianity and Buddhism there is the idea that there is nothing wrong with having comforts and possessions once people are free from desire for them. Life can be enjoyed with all its goodness if there is no attachment to it. Indeed, it can only be truly enjoyed when people are open to what comes without ambition or anxiety. Buddhism is the middle way between ascetic denial of the world and seeking satisfaction in and through the world. This is not difficult for Christians to understand.

But between most Christian quests for overcoming attachment to the world and the Buddhist teaching there remain deep differences. The Buddhist demand is more radical than anything found in the West. Christians have generally sought to overcome their baser desires for the sake of nobler ones. One struggles against selfish interests so as to come to pure love of the neighbor. One tries to free oneself from worldly attachments so as to devote oneself more completely to spiritual goals. Or, for the sake of eternal blessedness, one finds it eminently wise to give up temporal pleasures, especially as these turn sour even in the course of the present life.

One may find in some Buddhist teaching also a relative valuing of different ends. And this valuing may correspond generally with that of Christians. But this is not the heart of the message. One does not detach oneself from selfish goals in order to attach oneself to noble ideals or the good of others. Commitment and love in this sense ultimately bind one to the sphere of suffering as tightly as do lust and greed.

But does not the Buddhist at least desire to attain the goal of release from suffering? This corresponds to the spiritual and otherworldly goals sought by the Christian, and there is certainly a sense in which the Buddhist message presupposes the desire to attain it. If there were no such desire, there would be no reason to engage in the disciplines recommended by Gautama or to work to overcome craving for other things.

Nevertheless, unlike the usual formulations in the West, Buddhism calls on us to give up attachment as such, and totally. That includes the desire for freedom from suffering, or Nirvana. Nirvana cannot be attained as long as it is sought. It is only when this last and purest desire is extinguished that the goal is attained.

Christian teaching contains some similar paradoxes. Jesus warned us that we find life only by giving it up. In the New England theology it was taught that only those could be saved who were willing to be damned for the glory of God. But again these paradoxes do not penetrate as deeply as does the Buddhist one. It is for the sake of Christ or the neighbor that we lay down our lives. It is for the glory of God that the New England theologians taught we should be willing even to be damned. For the Buddhist, acts motivated in this way would still express attachment. Attachment to the neighbor, to Christ, or to God is still attachment, just as binding as any other. We are not called to give up lower attachments for higher ones but attachment itself, including the attachment to Nirvana which has first led us to be willing to surrender others. It would be hard to find in our Christian heritage the idea that we should give up our attachment to Christ. Yet from the Buddhist point of view this is absolutely necessary.

Insofar as Christianity teaches that we should cleave to Christ or devote ourselves wholly to God, Buddhism sees this teaching as an obstacle to release from suffering. It is for this reason, and not out of general intellectual skepticism, that Buddhists have either denied the reality of God or been silent on the subject. Belief in God affords profound temptation to attachment. Indeed, the idea of God is usually the idea of one to whom it is appropriate to cling or cleave. The worship of God is usually the expression of such an attitude. For that reason worship is not encouraged in Buddhism.

Because the Buddha can also so easily serve as an object of attachment, there is a famous Buddhist saying to the effect: If you meet the Buddha, kill him.

Buddhists have found that one of the most pervasive forms of attachment is the attachment to understanding. The mind seeks to grasp reality. Hence much of the best known work of Buddhist teachers is directed toward breaking this attachment. One meditates on the conceptually nonsensical or receives, in answer to an ordinary question, a kick. Disorientation is necessary if one is to break the habit of clinging to understanding.

This disorientation has another function. Language and culture have oriented us to an experience of the world that divides self and other. As long as we experience in that way, we cannot wholly free ourselves from attachment. That is, as long as there appears to be something to attach to and a self to attach to it, one never attains complete nonattachment. The destruction of that illusion is dealt with in the following section. The point here is that one will not escape the illusions which support attachment until one gives up attachment to those illusions. That involves giving up our desires for conceptual comprehension of the world even in simple and ordinary respects. For only when one surrenders all one's thinking processes can the world be for one what it in fact always is.

For Christians the service of Christ is perfect freedom. That usually means that through attachment to Christ we become free from all other attachments. The ability to live in the world and enjoy the world without being bound by the world is greatly prized by Christians.

The freedom which Buddhists find in complete nonattachment is even more fundamental and total. One is completely free *for* all things whatsoever because one is completely free *from* all things whatsoever. There is no bondage, not even to Christ or Buddha. One regrets nothing and one hopes for nothing. One strives for nothing and avoids nothing. Therefore one is completely present, completely without guilt or anxiety, and completely content.

To the Christian this sounds at first like a selfish goal. But in fact, far from being selfish it is wholly selfless. With the abandonment of all attachment the self disappears, for the self is part of the illusion generated by attachment. Being completely present, one is completely present for what needs to be done. One is perfectly compassionate. The Buddhist ideal is the salvation of all sentient creatures, not the separate salvation of individual people. The very idea of individual people is an illusion.

Buddhist practices appear anti-intellectual and irrational, and indeed they may be so. But the Buddhist goal is not ignorance or foolish behavior. The goal is wisdom. The point is that wisdom comes only when one ceases to cling to what people call knowledge and ability to think. Wisdom is the complete recognition of the world as it is and the response to that world which is in fact appropriate to it. All ordinary knowledge, thought, and conceptualization interfere with that world's self-revelation. Wisdom comes only as one lets that go.

In one sense Nirvana is a very simple matter. It is the absence of attachment, clinging, or craving. That absence gives rise to perfect freedom, perfect presence, perfect wisdom, and perfect compassion. There is no more to be said. Indeed, all the efforts to use conceptual thought to understand Nirvana are obstacles to its realization. On the other hand, to overcome attachment is so radical an alteration of our being that vast efforts have been expended on understanding how it is possible and what is involved. Some of these efforts are summarized in the sections that follow.

II. The Dissolution of Self as the Realization of True Self

Chapter Three showed that most nineteenth-century Westerners could conceive of the extinction of self and personal existence only as death. They were correct in thinking that mere death could not be the goal that inspired tens of millions of Buddhists, but with the exception of Schopenhauer they were powerless to grasp how else self and personal existence could be extinguished except, perhaps, by the absorption into deity that Buddhism clearly did not assert. We can escape this dilemma today, but it is still not easy for most Westerners to conceive as a supreme goal a nonpersonal existence in which selfhood is absent. Because it is important that more of us understand and appreciate what the Buddhists are saying here, I invite you to engage with me in a fresh adventure of thought.

Our question is the reality of the self. As we reflect about this the self is what is reflecting. So we must think about the self that is thinking about itself. Is it possible to think the thinker? Or must what we think about always be an object to the thinker? Must the thinker always be only a postulate which can never be directly thought at all?

Despite their verbal complexity, these are questions which lie close at hand even for those not accustomed to speculation. What do you think of when you think about yourself? Perhaps you think of your appearance to others as you learn of it in the mirror. In that case, it is evident that the "you" you think about is not identical with the "you" who thinks. Perhaps you think about how it will feel to be in some new situation. That brings the "you" thought about and the "you" who thinks closer together, because the "you" who thinks is also the "you" who feels. But in this case the present "you" is thinking about a future "you." Since it is possible to anticipate the future "you" and to remember the past "you," you may now try to think about the present "you," that is, try to think reflexively.

This is where the problem arises. To think about something requires a separation from or objectification of what is thought about. But it seems that the present thinker cannot objectify the present thinker. When one tries, one objectifies an idea about the present thinker instead.

The problem is not limited to thinking. Sense experience, memory, and anticipation all distinguish their data as objects from the one who senses, remembers, and anticipates. One cannot feel, remember, or anticipate oneself in the strict sense of the self who is now feeling, remembering, or anticipating. Is there, then, some other mode of self-relatedness in which the self is given to itself, so that in some sense it can be known?

One might respond that this is not so important. Even if I cannot catch myself in the moment of my act of knowing, sensing, remembering, or anticipating, I can nevertheless remember myself as knowing, sensing, remembering, and anticipating in moments that have just passed. In reflecting on these moments, one may suppose, I can grasp what my self is. One may argue that only an artificial skepticism can prevent me from attributing the same characteristics to my present self. Thus it seems that, by a slight detour, I can grasp my self.

But can I? Retrospective attention to my past self is attention to what is, for me now, an object. Further, it is attention to an object that did not know its self. I can retrospectively attend to its knowing, its sensing, its remembering, and its anticipating, but I cannot attend to its self, for that self was not part of the experience I am recalling. If I cannot know my self in the present, I cannot recall that self when, later, I look back upon this experience.

In the West we have generally responded to this elusiveness of the self by positing a self that underlies or transcends the knowing, feeling, remembering, and anticipating. This self is understood to be both the agent and the patient of this experience, both acting and acted upon. The Hindus also posited an underlying self but they taught that this true self is ultimately neither agent nor patient. It is not affected by the psychological flux. The Buddhists, on the other hand, denied the existence of any such self. There is a flow of experience but there is no self underlying or transcending it. These three responses have been fateful ones, not only for thought, but also for the structures of existence that have emerged. In Suzuki's words: "The individual ego asserts itself strongly in the West. In the East, there is no ego."[2] For Suzuki, of course, the absence of the ego is far better. This becomes clear as he proceeds to describe the differences more fully. Christianity, as he sees it, encourages combativeness and exclusiveness; it stirs, agitates, and disturbs. Buddhism, on the contrary, promotes peace, serenity, equanimity, equilibrium, broadmindedness, universal tolerance, and aloofness from worldly discriminations.[3] He sums up the difference in a striking image: "That Christ died vertically on the cross whereas Buddha passed away horizontally—does this not symbolize the fundamental difference . . . ?"[4]

Christians have been encouraged to act responsibly and to experience their emotions intensely. The central Christian symbol of the cross represents the denial of the self, but it also represents both heroic action and immeasurable passion. Jesus as perfect self is seen as totally involved in both. Even God is viewed as immersed in history through the incarnation. The result of such images in Christendom has been the formation of strong personalities aware of their sin and suffering, but also conscious of their significance as individuals and prizing the complexity of their inner lives and characters.

Hindu India has developed the most refined techniques for dissociation from the flux of action and passion. The world of action and passion is there, of course, but it is a world of secondary reality or even illusion. The true and sacred reality is realized by withdrawal from involvement in this secondary world into the changeless peace and blessedness of the true self that underlies and transcends it. This true self is one with all true selves and with ultimate reality as such. Accordingly, all differentiated personalization and individuality, together with the involvement in action and passion which they represent, are subordinated to the final ideal of mystical union.

Buddhism, especially in the forms that Mahayana assumed in China and Japan, achieved a middle way between active involvement and active withdrawal from the flux of events. Both involvement and withdrawal are based on a dualism of self and world which, Buddhists believe, distorts the actual situation. When we realize that actual situation, we find ourselves in the world, responding appropriately to it without either the Christian intensification of experience or the Hindu release. All craving is extinguished, even the craving to exist or not to exist. With the extinction of craving comes the cessation of suffering.

The question about the self is not, therefore, a matter of idle speculation. Our lives are shaped by conscious or unconscious answers to that question. Most people in the West still live by the inherited Western-Christian answer even when they no longer identify themselves as Christian. But there has been an inner Western development that has led to loss of confidence in that answer and to an experienced loss of self. On the whole, this has been felt as a threat and an abyss. But it has also opened the West to appreciation of the alternative answers of Hinduism and Buddhism. These no longer appear as obvious errors or primitive stages in the advance toward Western personhood. They appear instead as important and attractive alternatives for our own future.

For this reason it is worthwhile to pursue the Buddhist answer further. Have Buddhists, as they claim, discerned a way of being in the present through which the true nature of present selfhood becomes manifest? Does this lead, as Buddhists say, to blessedness, rather than to the abyss of meaninglessness and nihilism that the West fears? If so, does Buddhism offer the fulfillment the West vainly seeks in its own history? Would something of value and importance be lost if the West simply gave up its own heritage in favor of Buddhist enlightenment?

Buddhism offers primarily a system of disciplines through which adepts can realize their true situation and condition. Buddhists believe that only through such realization can Buddhist beliefs become fully intelligible and credible. Hence, it will be hard for those of us who have neither experienced enlightenment nor practiced the meditative disciplines which orient Buddhists to it to understand just what is involved. Still the effort of Buddhist thinkers is not to guard esoteric secrets but to explain as helpfully as possible what they have come to see. And in this time, when received habits of Western thought have become problematic, Westerners can grasp much of what they are saying.

Buddhism shows us first that in each moment there is no other reality than the subject experiencing. The subject may think of itself as in a world that is spread out in a space and time which contain many other subjects, but this idea is the subject's own construct. In the moment of its own immediacy it is absolutely alone in its immediacy. To exist at all is to exist in this way. There is no other existence than this momentary immersion in subjective immediacy. There is no perspective outside this immersion from which to view it. It itself is the only and universal perspective. The world of the subject experiencing is the only world there is.

But, as already noted, the subject or self is not present in the subject's world. That world is a world of objects and is exhausted by these objects. There is not, in addition to those objects, something else that is a subject. Hence it is as true to say that there are nothing but objects as that there is nothing but the subject. It is as true to say that there are no objects as that there is no subject.

The point of these paradoxes is not to exercise our dialectical capacities. The point is to show that there is no subject apart from objects and that there are no objects apart from a subject. This means that the ideas about objects and subjects with which we ordinarily reflect are confused. These ideas imply some kind of separate existence for objects and subject, some kind of mutual externality and independent substantiality. But what we actually have—or, better, *are*—are objects becoming subjects which become objects constituting new subjects. This process is not carried out by an agent, and it does not happen to anyone or to anything. It is not grounded in anything, and it cannot be contrasted with some other reality of a different sort. This process is the only self there is, hence, the true self, which is at once true reality.[5] The actual realization of this reality, as opposed to mere conceptual acknowledgment, is at once reality and blessedness. It is Nirvana.

III. Ultimate Reality as Emptiness

Nirvana names the Buddhist goal. In this way it corresponds to the kingdom of God in Jesus' proclamation. But despite some tendency to interiorize the kingdom and to view it as an eternal reality, the kingdom remains future. If it now exists, it does so proleptically. It is anticipated as the final consummation that God will give. Nirvana, on the other hand, is primarily nontemporal. The individual's realization or attainment of Nirvana may be future, but what is attained or realized is unaffected by this. Nirvana is primordial and ultimate, beyond all time and change.

In this respect Nirvana resembles more closely the Western God, especially as conceived by Aristotle. Aristotle's God draws all things toward itself as their end but is unaffected by their movement. But here, too, the difference is great. It is true that the highest human attainment for Aristotle is to contemplate God, but God remains a reality quite distinct from the one who contemplates. There is no realization or attainment of God as there is of Nirvana.

Esse or being, with which also Christians have identified God, is closer to Nirvana. Being, like Nirvana, is uncreated and indestructible. For being is that by virtue of which whatever exists exists at all.

Whatever the exact relation of being to Nirvana may be, there is no doubt that it is a peculiarly valuable bridge from the Western tradition to the East. It is unfortunate, therefore, that the concept of being has become so obscure for much of the West and especially for the English-speaking world. Chapter Three noted the work of Martin Heidegger in renewing the question of being. The following effort to use this Western tradition as a bridge to the understanding of Nirvana is indebted to this renewal although it makes no claim to reproduce his formulations.

Consider any object in your world. A chair will do. If we undertake to say what it is, we will describe its shape, texture, color, use, and so forth. But when we have completed our description, we still have said nothing that distinguishes this actual chair from an imaginary one. We will have listed qualities, attributes, universals, forms, or essences. These are all abstractions, and the combination of abstractions constitutes only a more complex abstraction. It does not constitute an existent or actual chair. We must add that in this case the combination of abstractions has been actualized.

What is this last step? Have we added to the other qualities one more which we call existence, actuality, reality, or being? No. If being were one more quality or essence, that would not do the trick. The difference between an imaginary and a real chair is not that one has an attribute lacking in the other. It is instead the difference between nonbeing and being, and that is a totally different kind of difference. Being is not one abstraction alongside others, but that which makes the difference between all abstractions and what is concrete. All other universals are abstractions, but this one, if we are to call it a universal at all, is concrete, or rather it is what gives concreteness to whatever is actual.

Of course, being is not an object or entity alongside others. It is the being of all objects or entities whatsoever, that by virtue of which they are. One cannot say where it is, for it is equally everywhere, and yet nowhere in the sense that objects are somewhere. One cannot say what it is, because every description is an attribution of some form, and being is neutral with respect to all forms. Being is not a thing, and in that sense it is nothing. Yet it is the act of being by virtue of which all beings are.

Now much of this could be said in a similar way of Nirvana. Both being and Nirvana are names for ultimate reality, but when this identify is recognized, more precise questioning becomes possible. First, can being function, as does Nirvana, as that whose realization or attainment is salvific? That question is not easy to answer, since in the Christian West salvation is not usually thought of in these terms. The kingdom of God is not identified with being so much as with a future community of persons among whom God's will is done. Still, the answer to the question is a qualified affirmative, for Western mystics have sought and attained union with being. In Meister Eckhart, for example, who follows St. Thomas's metaphysics closely, being or *esse* is identified with Godhead, and the highest peak of mystical experience is the realization of unity with Godhead.

The second question is whether the negative note in Nirvana is sufficiently grasped in the no-thing-ness and absence of form that characterize being. Suzuki seems little troubled by this, for he frequently cites Meister Eckhart as though Eckhart's mystical union with Godhead were the same as Buddhist realization of Nirvana. Yet the problem is not so easily resolved. Rudolf Otto has convincingly shown that being in Western terminology closely resembles Brahman in Hindu thought.[6] As noted in Chapter Three above, Otto displays the similarity of Eckhart and Sankara in their respective mystical experiences and interpretations. To identify Eckhart's experience also with the Buddhist one would imply the identity of Nirvana with Brahman. Hindus and Western mystics have tended to make this identification, but as long as Buddhism maintains its distinction from Hinduism, there is an affirmed or implied difference. Nirvana for the Buddhist is not identical with

Brahman. On the contrary, it is the negation of Brahman. Nirvana is Nothingness in a more radical sense than the no-thing-ness usually attributed to being in the West or Brahman in Hinduism.

In Western thought being is contrasted to all forms, attributes, or qualities as that by virtue of which they can be actualized. It thus underlies, grounds, and supports all things. In this sense it is viewed as the universal substance. But this sense of being as the unchanging substance underlying all changing things has become questionable in the West as well. Heidegger in particular has challenged what he calls the onto-theo-logical view of being. Instead, we should think of being as just what appears in the occurring of things—not as their substantial ground.

Buddhists, in rejecting Brahman in favor of Nirvana, are rejecting the quest for a ground or substratum to be found in ourselves that is one with the substantial being of all things. There is for Buddhists no such substance, hence no such being or Brahman. To name ultimate reality Nirvana is to deny it substantiality. Accordingly, Buddhist meditation is not in quest of the ground but of the dissolution of all grounds.

In subsequent centuries some Buddhists feared that there remained still a sense of substantiality to Nirvana by virtue of its contrast with Samsara, the world of ordinary things. All Buddhists had denied substantial reality to Samsara. This was the world of transmigration, of relativistic flux, of *pratitya-samutpada* or dependent origination. All things *are* only by their participation in other things. No thing has any existence in itself. But if Nirvana is juxtaposed to Samsara as its opposite, then to Nirvana as ultimate reality seems to be attributed an independent and self-contained existence. Even though Nirvana was not conceived as the substance of the world, it was in danger of being seen as self-existent, or *sva-bhava*.

This duality of a self-contained Nirvana and a relativistic flux expressed an incompleteness in the attainment of true understanding, and hence, in its turn, it was denied in Mahayana Buddhism. Nirvana and Samsara are not two different spheres or states, they are one. Nirvana is *sunya*, or empty, just as Samsara is. Nirvana is Samsara and Samsara is Nirvana. The realization of the one is at once the realization of the other. What is realized is *Sunyata* or Emptiness, which for much of Mahayana becomes the preferred way of naming ultimate reality.

Emptiness is not to be understood as a vacuum carefully shut off from the surrounding plenum. It is just the reverse. The idea of such a vacuum suggests precisely the self-existence which is wholly illusory. To be empty is to lack any boundaries, any determining content of one's own, any filter through which the world is experienced. To be empty is to be perfectly open to what is there, whatever that may be. It is to be completely defenseless and with nothing to defend. One is then perfectly full, for one is constituted by the dependent origination of the whole world. This process is ultimate reality, at once Nirvana and Samsara. This is quite different from the usual Western understanding of being!

Western reflection on being provides a bridge to pass over to a conceptual understanding of Nirvana and even to grasp its negative element, its opposition to all substantial conceptions of ultimate reality. But when one crosses the bridge, the experience of reality changes radically. Ultimate reality is no longer God. The realization of Emptiness is not the union of the soul with God or the realizaton of the oneness of Atman and Brahman. There are for the Buddhist no soul and no God to unite, no Atman and no Brahman whose oneness can be attained. There is only Emptiness, whose realization is perfect peace.

IV. The Abolition of Time and History

A third approach to understanding Nirvana will overlap with the others and converge upon the same conclusion, but in the process it can both cast further light on Nirvana and raise additional challenges to ordinary Western thinking. What does Nirvana mean for time-consciousness, the sense of past, present, and future? And how does it relate to the Western habit of orienting life by a picture of the course of historical events?

The dominant Christian experience of time is one of transcendence. As agent self or responsible actor, one is in time specifically by being in the present moment. But one is also beyond that moment in the sense that, in one's awareness of being here-now, one objectifies here-now from some other perspective. One remembers anticipating this moment and anticipates remembering it. One brings into this moment responsibility for what one has been and responsibility for the projects one will bequeath to one's future. The meaning of the present moment derives from what has been and from what is to be.

In some instances, as in a conversation with a chance traveling companion, the past and future that are the primary context giving meaning to successive moments are quite limited. Yet the primary context is set in the larger context of the whole trip and of one's continuing life. The self who speaks in the moment is the self who has been shaped by one's whole biography and by the anticipation of future experience. Further, even one's personal life and destiny cannot supply an adequate context. These are bound up with family and friends and the wider society. What one does receives its meaning from history as well as biography. How one perceives one's historical past and future determines the most general and also the most fundamental grounds for the meaning of each fleeting moment. Hence the meaning and context of the moment derive precisely from our transcendence of that moment in that moment. That is, a crucial aspect of the momentary experience is its imaginative self-objectification as a part of a vast sweep of time.

This orientation of itself in time makes Christian experience fundamentally historical. What is possible and desirable for an American citizen in the late twentieth century is profoundly different from what was possible and desirable for a German knight in the fourteenth century. To be responsible is to orient oneself rightly in the historical matrix. The correct interpretation of history is the foundation of ethical action and personal meaning. This makes knowledge about the past and projections of probable futures fundamentally important to Christian civilization. It makes factual knowledge, including scientific knowledge, religiously important.

The Buddhist by no means denies that human beings tend to transcend themselves in this way. We do, and this is the root source of our suffering. We identify ourselves with what we have done and been in the past and thereby encumber ourselves with guilt. We anticipate future evils and thereby fill ourselves with anxiety. These impose structures upon what is experienced instead of allowing the experience to be what it is. This whole process of self-transcendence thus prevents us from truly living and authentically experiencing in the moment.

Moreover, there is no other time at which true and authentic fulfillment can occur. There are only here-nows. The past is gone and the future is not yet. When the past was present, it consisted in such moments of living experience, and when the present passes, there will be only additional such moments. To live now from the past does nothing for the past. To subordinate the present to the future is to forgo salvation forever; for there will never be a future—only a new present. What will be possible in the new present is already possible in this one.

The Buddhist points out that the Western habit of historical orientation presupposes that history has some meaning. That is, the differences between our time and the fourteenth century—or the fifth century B.C.—are genuinely important only if they relate to the meaning or purpose of human existence. But they can relate to these basic issues only if history has a goal or destiny. Otherwise, every moment is "equidistant from eternity," and in relation to the human goal, the temporal location is indifferent.

There is no doubt that belief in destiny has underlain our Western consciousness of time. It is central to both Judaism and Christianity. Since the eighteenth century, Jewish expectation of the coming of the Messiah and Christian expectation of the second coming of Christ have waned, but these have been replaced by secular hopes. The vision of universal democracy, education, prosperity, and peace as well as that of the classless society renewed for many advanced Western thinkers the sense of the imminence of the consummation of history.

Buddhists perceive Judeo-Christian and secularized expectations as alike illusory. There are changes in the outward course of events, but these do not lead anywhere. There will be no consummation. Hence we cannot orient ourselves in relation to a Beginning and an End. Against the Western sense of six thousand years of history, the Buddhist thinks of human events as continuing for millions upon millions of years, even forever. There is no origin and no conclusion. The patterns the West can find in its short history are trivialized in the vast temporal distances of the Buddhist vision. Further, this planet, which the Western imagination has regarded as the center of all things, is but one of millions of worlds for the Buddhist. Hence, to orient our lives to the course of human events on this planet is an illusion.

Modern science treats both Western and Buddhist views as exaggerations. From its point of view the Western time scheme is ludicrously foreshortened; but time and change, and the particularity of the earth as the home of human beings, retain an importance in the usual scientific view that is in tension with the Buddhist vision as well.

Factual accuracy of the two visions, however, is not the time issue. Christians can acknowledge that the universe is far older than earlier supposed and still orient life to the six thousand years of civilized history. Buddhists can acknowledge that their traditions have underestimated the degree of evolutionary change that has occurred without finding in the scientific picture anything to shake their conviction that fundamental human meaning cannot be gained by orientation to the outer course of events.

Buddhists like to quote a saying deriving ultimately from the third-century Corpus Hermeticum to the effect that the center is everywhere; the circumference is nowhere.[7] Precisely because there is no beginning or end and no spatial boundary, every point anywhere in space and time is equally the center of the whole. Every other point is located in relation to it. When the effort to order the infinite flux is abandoned, the here-now is accepted as the only possible principle of orientation.

The habit of self-transcendence is fed by another illusion as well. Even when we verbally admit that we are immersed in time, we do so as if we were also observers viewing this immersion from without. This habit is recognized in the West as well. For example,

Rilke wrote: "And we spectators, always, everywhere, looking at, never out of, everything!"[8] This outside perspective blocks the full realization of the meaning of the initial Western admission that we are immersed in time. One thinks about being immersed in time as if there were some other possibility, as if one could be somehow detached from the immersion.

In these ways, one wards off the ultimate truth that reality is simply the immediacy of momentary being or becoming, in which each ingredient is just what it is as that ingredient in that momentary becoming. There may be memories, anticipations, and concepts, but they are features of the momentary becoming just as are emotions and sensations and intuitions. They do not remove us from the moment. When this is realized, their power to structure other aspects of experience is broken.

The result for the Buddhist is not the barren emptiness that is so feared by Westerners but an Emptiness of perfect receptivity and spontaneity. The disorganization of experience allows each ingredient to be itself, evoking only that response that is appropriate to it. The empty moment becomes by its Emptiness the full moment, perfect in itself, and released from involvement with either past or future.

The Buddhist analysis assaults our Western time-consciousness one step further. Not only can the here-now not orient itself toward an inclusive history, but in its own moment of occurrence, it is not temporal at all. Within it there is neither past nor future, neither has-been nor not-yet. The here-now is complete and perfect in itself. Furthermore, there is not some other, temporal, reality to contrast with the non-temporal here-now. What-is is always and necessarily here-now. Time exists only for the perspective that objectifies the here-now and views the succession of moments as if from without. But ultimately there is no such perspective. When this illusoriness of time is experientially realized, time is existentially dissolved. The distinction of past from future and of both from present has only the reality given it by the illusory self-transcendence of the here-now. All such distinctions disappear in the completely fulfilled moment which is Nirvana.

NOTES

1. This is the subject of the sermon at Benares on the Four Noble Truths. The sermon, which is attributed to Gautama shortly after his enlightenment, may be found in various collections of Buddhist writings. See, for example, *The Teachings of the Compassionate Buddha*, ed. E. A. Burtt (New York: Mentor Books, 1955), pp. 29–32.

2. Daisetz Teitarō Suzuki, *Mysticism: Christian and Buddhist* (New York: Harper & Bros., 1957), p. 129.

3. Ibid., pp. 137–39.

4. Ibid., p. 137.

5. I have been guided in this exposition by Yoshifumi Ueda, "The Status of the Individual in Mahayana Buddhist Philosophy," in *The Japanese Mind: Essentials of Japanese Philosophy and Culture*, ed. Charles A. Moore (Honolulu: University of Hawaii Press, 1967).

6. Otto, *Mysticism East and West.*

7. See the Preface by André Maurois to Jorge Luis Borges, *Labyrinths* (New York: New Directions, 1962), pp. ix–x.

8. Cited by Thomas Merton, *Mystics and Zen Masters* (New York: Dell Publishing Co., 1967), p. 245.

CHAPTER FIVE

Coming Back

IN CHAPTER FOUR I SUMMARIZED the Buddhist's understanding of Nirvana. I presented the ideas as persuasively as I could because I myself find them convincing. But I also presented them in sharp contrast with characteristic Christian ways of thinking about comparable matters because we are too likely to neglect the differences. In fact the contrast between Buddhist and Christian teaching often appears as a virtual contradiction. It seems that to accept the Buddhist vision must involve repudiation of the Christian one. It appears as though one must choose between Buddhism and Christianity. It seems that if one once crosses over one cannot come back.

This chapter argues that in the end such a choice will not prove necessary. Christians can learn from Buddhism without ceasing to be Christians. In William Johnston's words, Christianity "will find her encounter with the Orient no less enriching than her meeting with Greco-Roman thought."[1] By allowing itself to be transformed in this way, Christianity can convert the apparent contradictions into complementary contrasts. In all their differences, the truth of Buddhism and the truth of Christianity can live together.

The Christianity that has appropriated and incorporated the Buddhist understanding of reality will not be the same as the Christianity shaped by its long experience in the West. The task of this chapter is to show some of the new forms that it will need to take.

The question of incorporating Buddhist wisdom into Christian faith is not a merely theoretical one. The effort is proceeding on a practical level, too. Merton's support and example stimulated the practice of Zen in Catholic monasteries in the United States. Father Enomiya LaSalle established a Catholic Zen Center near

Tokyo where Zen has been extensively adapted to Christian use. Japanese Catholics, such as Father Kadowaki, have entered deeply into the practice of Zen, approaching its mastery. In doing so they are continuing a tradition of Japanese Christians of the Meiji era who tried to retain and deepen their Buddhism through the Christian faith in a time when the Buddhist leadership was intensely hostile to Christianity.

On the Protestant side Katsumi Takizawa studied under Karl Barth and was baptized as a Christian without rejecting the deeply Buddhist philosophy in which he had been trained. More recently the Christian New Testament scholar, Seiichi Yagi, has discovered the power and truth of Buddhist wisdom and transformed his Christian understanding through it. Takizawa and Yagi have written major and widely read books on Christianity and Buddhism which have intensified the discussion as to the possibility and nature of a Buddhist Christianity.

The fact that these experiments are occurring does not mean that the question is settled. Far from it. The practice of Zen meditation can have so powerful an effect that rather than contributing, as Merton and Johnston have hoped, to a deepening of Christianity it can lead to its dissolution. Indeed, there must be serious doubt as to whether one who has really experienced the full force of Buddhist liberation can ever again take an interest in the central themes of Christian faith. Having passed over, in this case, there may be no way of coming back.

Indeed, the strongest warnings come from those who have passed over. Francis Cook has written: "The radical nature of emptiness is apparent when it is said that we must even empty emptiness, leaving us with no conceptual mediary between our subjectivity and the experienced world. Consequently in authentic emptiness as experience, we are left with no conceptual props, including emptiness itself. How much more must this be true of such things as history, selfhood, God, and so forth? . . . On the experiential level, where it really counts, emptiness seems to be completely incompatible with certain Christian concerns."[2]

Whether this incompatibility is the final word or whether, as Johnston suggests, "through Zen we may . . . find a new approach to Christ, an approach that is less dualistic and more Oriental"[3] cannot yet be determined. As Johnston noted, the experience of the Buddhist practitioner of Zen and that of the Christian practitioner of Zen are not identical. Experience, even this purest of experience, is not wholly independent of the beliefs and ideas of the practitioner. That means that there is a role for conceptual reflection as well as disciplined practice. This chapter operates at that conceptual level. It inquires not whether Christianity is existentially compatible with the realization of Emptiness and of the emptiness of Emptiness, but whether Christian doctrine can be reformulated so as to take account of the fact that all things are empty. If it can, then the experience of Christians practicing Zen may be subtly affected by the transformed beliefs which they bring to their practice. The possibility of passing over to authentic Buddhist experience and coming back to Christian faith may be enhanced. But whether this will occur or not, there is for the Christian an intrinsic importance in incorporating what is conceptually learned from Buddhism into new formulations of Christian belief.

This chapter is a theological response to what has been learned in dialogue with Mahayana Buddhists. It illustrates what it means to go beyond dialogue. It is organized around the same four themes as the previous chapter, considering now in each case the possibility of a Christian response that has assimilated the truth of the Buddhist insight. Hence the four sections are provisional responses to the following questions. I. Can a Christian surrender all attachment, craving, and clinging even to Christ? II. Can a Christian accept as a goal the dissolution of personal existence? III. Can a Christian appropriate the vision of ultimate reality as Emptiness? IV. Can a Christian enter fully into the sheer immanence of the moment?

I. Faith Without Attachment

Chapter Four described the Buddhist call for the cessation of all desire and attachment. As applied to worldly pleasures and success this call is easy for the Christian to understand, however difficult it may be to obey. But Buddhism goes far beyond this. We are told that we must give up our attachment to Christ as well. At this point our central understanding of Christian faith is challenged. Are we not called to long for Christ, to forsake all else for Christ's sake, to put our trust only in Christ, in short, to cling to Christ alone? Is not faith itself a cleaving to Christ?

Indeed, from the Buddhist standpoint the usual Christian account of faith seems to present it as a form of clinging. According to Buddhist teaching, such clinging is exactly what keeps us in bondage. From Gautama on, Buddhist doctrine is the explanation of how to let go of all clinging to gain release from suffering. Once one has crossed over to a real appreciation of the enslaving character of clinging can one come back to Christian faith?

Although attachment and clinging do characterize most of what Christians have experienced as faith, there are important countercurrents within Christianity which move away from these attitudes. Furthermore, the idea of faith plays an important and positive role in Buddhism as well as in Christianity. The Christian encounter with Buddhism may enable Christians to come to a deeper understanding of faith.

The idea of faith is present in all forms of Buddhism. For example, if one seeks enlightenment under the direction of a Zen master, one must put one's faith in that master. One must be prepared to follow the master's directions, even when they seem absurd, without demanding an explanation. Further, one must have faith that Buddhism is a true witness to the nature of reality, that Nirvana is rightly pointed to in its teaching, and that enlightenment is a possibility for human beings. Apart from this fundamentally trusting and believing attitude, no one would proceed through the intense disciplines of Zen.

At a still deeper level, there must be faith in ultimate reality itself. Although one practices special disciplines and austerities in order that enlightenment may come, one is enlightened, not by these efforts, but by ultimate reality itself; and one must trust this reality to do what it alone can do. Enlightenment breaks in upon one as though from beyond; it is not constructed by personal effort. There can be no enlightenment as long as the ego is in control.

Nevertheless, Christians are not wrong in sensing that what is meant by faith here is quite different from what Christians mean by faith. In Christian faith, that in which one believes never ceases to be other even when it is most fully embodied. God's immediacy can be so decisive that Paul can write of the new life after being crucified with Christ as the life of Christ within him. Still, the distinction between believers and the One who lives within them remains (Gal. 2:20). I am not God, and God is not me. In Zen, on the other hand, the Other in which one places one's faith is at the same time one's own true self. Enlightenment is the realization that what one seeks is what one has always been.

Not only is the otherness of that in which one believes overcome in the attainment of the Zen goal, but also the attitude of faith is essentially superseded. Faith is needed to hold us to the road and open us to enlightenment, but in enlightenment itself, faith disappears. When the truth is realized,one no longer needs to trust the teacher or the teaching; for one knows for oneself. In fact, one *is* the knowledge. Despite its great importance, faith cannot be inherent in salvation itself.

Nevertheless, not all Buddhists share this rejection of otherness in the object of faith or the accompanying idea that faith is left behind. Pure Land Buddhism, indeed, criticizes Zen for its reliance on self-power and calls instead for faith in the other-power of the Buddha, Amida.[4] In twelfth-century Japan the monk, Hōnen, became persuaded that in our corrupt age the only successful road to enlightenment is through complete dependence on Amida. Hence he recommended to everyone the recitation of Amida's name, the *Nembutsu*, as the sole practice. Of course, the name must be recited in the right attitude of sincerity and faith.

Many Christians understand faith in a way not unlike that of Hōnen. They believe that if they participate in Christian practices, such as the sacraments, prayer, and Bible reading, or the recitation of the rosary, with an attitude of sincerity and faith, they will be saved. They understand God's grace as God's gift of these means of salvation, which frees them from the need to seek salvation through arduous practices or perfect virtue. The issue between this kind of Buddhism and this kind of Christianity is whether the recitation of the *Nembutsu* or one or another of these Christian practices is in fact the best means of salvation.

Nevertheless, both in Christianity and in Pure Land Buddhism, there is a deeper understanding of faith responding to similar problems in the two traditions. Luther realized that as long as his salvation depended on a right mental and spiritual attitude on his own part, it remained forever uncertain. He could not be sure of his own sincerity and faith. Given these requirements there can be no human assurance of salvation. Luther's biblical study persuaded him that we are not saved by the correctness of our attitude but by an unconditional, utterly free, gift of God in Jesus Christ. Thus faith is not a state of mind which one must work to produce in oneself. It is itself a part of the divine gift. The good news is that we are saved apart from any achievement on our own part, even and especially the achievement of sincerity and faith.

Shinran, one of the disciples of Hōnen, came to a remarkably similar insight.[5] He had sought his salvation through difficult disciplines, and he felt that he had totally failed. Hence he heard the message of Hōnen with enthusiasm. But he understood Hōnen more radically than Hōnen understood himself.

Some of the disciples of Hōnen were fearful that at the crucial moment, the moment of death, they might lack the proper attitude of sincere faith. This showed that for them Pure Land teaching was still only an easier way of meeting the requirements of salvation. Shinran taught, in contrast, that it is not the human accomplishment of the right attitude that saves, but Amida's grace. Sinful human beings can be confident of salvation precisely because it is effected by Amida and not by human merit.[6]

Despite the remarkable and often noted similarities between Shinran and Luther, there are apparent differences between them in the meaning of faith. For Luther faith is almost identical with trust, whereas Shinran's word, *shinjin*, translated into English as "faith," means believing heart or mind. In certain respects this term and the Buddhist context of Shinran's thought drew his understanding of faith away from the usual Christian view.

Although Shinran emphasized trust in Amida, the accent falls on a state of being or consciousness rather than on an interpersonal relation. The Other Power in whom one trusts is not imaged finally as outside us in the way another person would be, but as the true principle or depth of our own being. Not only is faith pure gift but in an important sense faith is the realization of this other. The gift is the giver. Thus, although in the initial presentation and acceptance the accent falls on relation to the Other Power, the deepening of the understanding leads toward an identity of that Other with the state of being which it promises and bestows.

In Christianity the dominant imagery is certainly interpersonal, so that trust in a human friend can be used as a strong analogy for faith in Christ. If this imagery is essential to the deepest grasp of faith in Christ, then Shinran's faith must be recognized as something different. But this is not the case. The grace that works faith in our hearts is at once the Other and the Other's presence. Our faith is not only a relation to the source of grace but also the believing heart which that grace effects by its presence. In the deepening of faith the imagery often shifts from that of I and Thou to that of the indwelling of Christ or the Holy Spirit. Though there is no final identity of self and Other, the Other is constitutive of the self.

We need not conclude that interpersonal imagery is inappropriate to the understanding of faith in either Jōdoshinshū, the denomination founded by Shinran, or in Lutheranism. But we can conclude that the poles of trust in a personal Other and participation in a state of being are found in both traditions. As such they are not barriers to recognition of a common meaning of faith in the two traditions. In each tradition there remains a need to clarify how these poles can be most fruitfully related, and in this effort of clarification each can aid the other.

Buddhist thinkers in the Zen tradition may still object that faith, whether in Christianity or in Pure Land Buddhism, involves some element of attachment or clinging even when the dualism of believer and God, so characteristic of Christian imagery, is overcome. It still involves some kind of holding fast, of selective attention, of focusing of hope and desire. And there is no doubt that this is true for ordinary believing. But similar elements can be found in Zen, also, up until the final enlightenment. They represent the imperfection of faith rather than its essential nature.

Perfect faith is complete letting go, not holding fast. Instead of controlling and directing attention, it is openness to whatever happens. Even its hope is the hope given by God in the moment rather than a hope nursed and nourished by the self and then grounded in God.

Even a Christianity which has learned from its encounter with Buddhism fully to reject faith as attachment in favor of faith as openness will differ from Zen. It will resemble Pure Land Buddhism more closely. But even here there will be differences. These need not arise out of the Christian's "clinging" faith which is overcome in Pure Land. They arise instead out of the different views of self, of God, and of history to which the remainder of this chapter is devoted.

II. The Dissolution and Transcendence of Personal Existence

Buddhist analysis dissolves the illusion of substantial self. It shows that there is no subject apart from objects and no objects apart from the subject. The subject is the coalescence of objects, and the objects exist only in that coalescence. There is no place for a self that exists in itself over against the world.

There can be no doubt that what is denied in this analysis is commonly affirmed in Christian and humanistic Western thought. The self as agent and patient has been distinguished from the flux of actions and events. It has been conceived as identical with itself through time. In short, the self has generally been conceived substantially. If Christians are required to affirm a substantial self, then Christianity and Buddhism are irreconcilably opposed to one another.

It is far from evident, however, that Christianity is bound up with a philosophical idea of this kind. Certainly this idea is not found in the Bible, and it is now widely recognized that, in general, much of our biblical heritage has been obscured by the more static and substantial categories through which the Greek influence has led us to read it. Recent Western philosophies have on the whole moved away from substantialist modes of thought and are more congenial than ever before to Buddhist ways of thinking.

On the other hand, it is true that Christianity has strengthened the self or ego, as Suzuki notes. We have been encouraged to assume responsibility for our actions and even for our motivations. We have experienced this call to responsibility as evoking our sense of freedom and drawing us out of collective security into personal individuality. It has become important to us that we not simply receive events passively or react to them mechanically. Instead we want to analyze our situation, identify its evils, project improvements, and invest ourselves in appropriate plans and programs. The self that is involved in all of this need not be substantial, but it is nevertheless real and strong, and the Buddhist dissolution of this mode of existence is certainly not aimed at encouraging the development of this Christian self. The Christian self, even when it is recognized not to be substantial, cannot be identified with the no-self or true-self of Buddhism.

We confront here two questions. First, can we understand the Christian self as real in light of the Buddhist dissolution of the illusory substantial self, or must we acknowledge that it, too, is illusory? Second, is there a way in which the Christian can appropriate the existential meaning of the Buddhist dissolution of the self without abandoning the achievement of the Christian self?

Let us return to the basic Buddhist vision of reality. Each momentary human experience is an instance of dependent origination, that is, of objects coalescing into a subject. There is no self that pre-exists this coalescence or underlies it. If there is a self at all it must emerge in the coalescence. For the Buddhist the true self is the coalescence as such, but this is not satisfactory for the Christian, for the coalescence as a whole does not have the responsible freedom that is definitive for the Christian self.

This issue of responsible freedom is not a traditional Buddhist one. With all their subtle discussions of philosophical topics, Buddhists have not treated the old Western question of freedom and determinism. Their talk of dependent origination often sounds deterministic to Western ears, but when contemporary Buddhists are confronted with this Western question, they consistently reject a rigid determinism. Still, they have yet to direct their attention to clarification of how an instance of dependent origination may involve an element of responsible freedom. It is not, for them, an important question.

The Christian who accepts the basic Buddhist analysis is more urgently pressed to discuss this question. If we conceive the coalescing elements as all alike actual, there is no room for freedom. The coalescence could only be a composite. Even if a factor of chance were allowed in the exact form of the composition, this would not help. Freedom is a matter not of chance but of self-determination through decision. Freedom may be compatible with sheer chance, but it is not facilitated or explained by it. Decision is a matter of selection among significant possibilities, and this can happen only if possibilities as such are elements in the coalescence. The presence of possibilities would mean that the coalescence is not a mere product of the actual world. It does or can introduce elements that are not derived from that world. *Whether* such elements are included and, if so, *which*, are decided only in the coalescence itself. That decision must express some immanent intention, goal, or aim guiding the coalescence. In this way we can conceive of an instance of dependent origination as determining freely and responsibly its own mode of integrating the elements by whose coalescence it is constituted.

In human experience we can also see that the sense of freedom will be correlated with the prominence of possibilities in distinction from actualities in the coalescence. In a culture that is not attentive to unrealized possibilities, responsible freedom will not be accented. On the other hand, where people are constantly urged to transcend the past toward a new and better future and to assume responsibility for how they confront the ever new possibilities of life, responsible freedom will be a prominent feature of reflection and actual existence. The Christian self is the decision-making element in the coalescence.

Buddhists know that in all ordinary experience these momentary instances of dependent origination are particularly dependent on past instances that through their succession constitute the personal life. The usual formulation of the doctrine of *karma* attests to the extent to which what occurs in one moment of experience is viewed by Buddhists as a product of the personal past. The quality of feeling and habits of thought and response that are inherited from this past dominate the instance of dependent origination that is the present experience. Similarly the decision-making element in the coalescence is ordinarily the contribution of this past.

Buddhists distinguish good *karma* from bad *karma*, but they nevertheless seek release from all *karma*. That is, they want the present instance of dependent origination to be free from this bondage to past personal experience. Only so can it be open to the totality of all that is, without discrimination and distortion. Hence the continuity of selfhood as the determinant of decision inherited through personal experience is viewed as a limitation to be overcome. Even if Buddhists could affirm the self as the decision in each concrescence, they would reject the personal self that links the momentary selves into a chain that endures through time.

For Christians, too, there is a sense that the determination of our decisions by the dominant aims derived from our past is unsatisfactory. We are taught not simply to seek to effect our best purposes but also to allow our purposes themselves to be transformed by Christ. The strong personal self which characterizes us is also the sinner who refuses to respond, moment by moment, to the call of Christ. The dominance of our past purposes restricts our openness to the new possibilities that are given by Christ. Hence it is not hard to understand and approve the Buddhist effort to become free from the dominance of one's own past. In opening ourselves to Christ we, too, seek that freedom.

Nevertheless, we appraise the relation to the personal past differently. For us it represents a peculiar and unique accumulation of experience that enables the new experiences that inherit from it to make distinctive contributions to the whole. To reduce the contribution of that personal life to my present experience would be to reduce my chance of rich and significant experience now. Even the evil and destructive elements in my past experience, insofar as they are healed and transformed by repentance, are capable of contributing something. The goal is not, therefore, to reduce the inheritance from the personal past but to allow the possibilities given now by Christ to order this inheritance. The Christian goal, therefore, is not the dissolution of the personal self but its continual transcending of the past through conformation to the ever new purposes of God.

Thus far I have given an affirmative answer to the first of the two questions. The theoretically accurate dissolution of the substantial self by Buddhist analysis, far from denying the possible reality of the Christian self, helps us to understand that self better. But the Christian goal is quite different from the Buddhist one. It is now time to deal with the second question. Can the Christian appropriate the existential meaning of the actual dissolution of the personal self, which is the Buddhist response to the theoretical dissolution of the substantial self?

Although Christians often cling to the personal self, we are not oblivious of its problems. The personal self constitutes itself in its individuality over against other personal selves. There is a strong experience of mutual externality. Mutual isolation is hardly overcome in Christian community. Furthermore, the call to love others as we love ourselves is experienced either as a remote and hardly relevant ideal, a burdensome and guilt-producing law, or as a supernatural gift. Relations to other persons are so different from relations to oneself that an equality of love is virtually inconceivable. One can at best have general good will and translate that into just actions and the refusal to favor oneself. Even this is a principle honored more in the breach than in the observance.

In Buddhism we see a profoundly different solution to the problem, one that fulfills many of our own ideals. As each momentary experience is freed both from bondage to a personal past and special orientation to a personal future, it becomes open to the whole world. It can respond to each element in that world appropriately, without the distortion of self-interest. And it can constitute itself with a view to the benefit of all without preoccupation with its own personal future. The barriers between persons, the mutual externality, disappear. Each participates in the other as in itself. The Christian commandment to love the neighbor as the self is transformed in the enlightened ones into a description of the actual relationship to others.

All of this cannot but be attractive to Christians, but it is attained at the price of a personal selfhood which we regard as precious. We are driven to ask whether there is not some way in which we can incorporate the Buddhist achievement without this sacrifice. Can we continue to be responsible personal selves and yet attain a measure of the impartial love of the enlightened Buddhist?

A first step in this direction is given by the acceptance of the original Buddhist analysis. The problems of mutual externality and isolation and the sense of the radical difference between the relation to the neighbor and the relation to the self have all been accentuated in the past by Western substantialist conceptualization. If each were in truth a separate substance, then indeed the relations to self would be wholly internal whereas the relations to others would be wholly external. The love commandment would then fly in the face of metaphysics! Community could only be the alongsidedness of several substances, each sealed off from real relations with the others. Obviously that is a caricature of the conclusions actually drawn from substantialist views of the self, but a caricature also has its truth. The way we have thought about ourselves and our relations has been in profound tension with the New Testament teaching of love and mutual participation.

The substantialist view is false. Moment by moment each self comes into being as a coalescence of elements that include others as well as the personal past. The personal past may dominate the coalescence, but the mode of relation that one such instance of dependent origination has to instances in its personal past is not different in kind from the mode of relation it has to other instances elsewhere. To think of the self in this way and then to realize experientially the reality of participation in one another can move Christians toward the Buddhist achievement.

This movement would not be toward the dissolution of the personal structure of existence, but it would be toward its transcendence. The difference is important for the Christian. The annihilation of personal selfhood is the breaking of the powerful and dominating influence of the personal past. Its transcendence is the development of relations to others that are increasingly able to inherit from them in ways that are like the way one inherits one's own past. If one now has almost perfect empathy for one's own immediate past, one can increase the degree of empathy one has for others. If one is now open to ideas that one has had in the past because they are one's own and is defensive toward the ideas of others, one can become increasingly open to ideas that come from others and more critical of one's own. If one now cares about one's future happiness, and constitutes one's present reality so as to contribute to it, one can also care about the happiness of others and constitute one's present reality to contribute to that as well.

The Buddhist transformation of experience is profound and inconceivable. I have suggested steps in the direction of a transformation of Christian experience that are modest and tentative in comparison. Perhaps a transformation is possible in the direction of transcending personal existence that is as dramatic and unimaginable as the Buddhist transformation in the direction of dissolution. If so, the resulting Christian experience might subsume the Buddhist experience within itself without ceasing to be Christian.

III. God and Emptiness

If ultimate reality is Emptiness, is the Christian forced to choose between identifying God with Emptiness and denying God altogether? If so, then the Christian must resist the recognition that ultimate reality is Emptiness. For the more fully Emptiness is understood, the clearer it becomes that it does not mean what the Bible means by God.

Another response is possible. The dissolution of the traditional

Western concept of being into Emptiness exposes the tensions that were always present in the identification of God with being. For being to be God it must be the source, cause, depth, or ground of being. To this being or ground of being must be attributed pure and perfect being. Hence, if God is identified with being, then being must be at once the being of beings, the ground of being, and the Supreme Being. This is conceptually confusing.

The tension between God and being is clear when we consider the parallel vision in Hinduism, where it was more easily resolved. There, Being Itself as Brahman manifests itself as the Lord, Isvara, the Supreme Being. There were tensions between those devoted to Isvara who denied the ultimate primacy of Brahman and those who asserted that Isvara's reality was subordinate to that of Brahman or even denied Isvara's ultimate reality. In either case, Brahman and Isvara are distinguished, and in India this distinction between ultimate reality and the personal God of the devotee could be acknowledged without embarrassment. In the West the same distinction has occasionally appeared between Godhead and God, but it has been resisted for its apparent tendency to subordinate God.

Despite exceptions which will be important for Chapter Six, wherever the distinction has been made there has been a strong tendency to subordinate the particular manifestation to the ultimate reality it manifests. This subordination is marked in Buddhism. Each Buddha manifests the Buddha-principle, the Buddha-nature, ultimate reality, or Emptiness. These manifestations are revered and even worshiped. But for most Buddhists the goal is not to attain the right relation to a Buddha but to realize what the Buddhas have realized, namely, ultimate reality.

The distinction of ultimate reality from its divine manifestations indicates a direction and sounds a warning for Christian faith. The direction is to accept without hesitation or embarrassment the distinction between ultimate reality and God, and to recognize that the God of the Bible, like Isvara and the Buddhas, is a manifestation of ultimate reality, not the name of that reality. The warning is that this relationship must be carefully formulated to avoid the tendency to subordinate the manifestation to what it manifests or to view what is manifested as "above" or "beyond" its manifestation in God.

Part of the problem is associated with the idea of manifestation itself. What is manifested would seem almost by definition to be prior and superior to its manifestations. Does "manifest," then, rightly describe God's relation to ultimate reality? Certainly God *does* manifest ultimate reality, but God also actualizes and embodies that reality. In the Christian view, God's supreme and adequate actualization of ultimate reality grounds the possibility of our creaturely actualizations. "Manifestation" alone does not express this relation.

Acceptance of the view that the ultimate reality is Emptiness rather than being can free us from the tendency to place it at the top of a hierarchy in which its actualizations are located in ontologically subordinate roles. When we think of being in the West and Brahman in India, the note of supreme actuality as well as reality is still heard, if confusedly. But Emptiness, while the supreme reality for Buddhists, is wholly devoid of actuality. People have worshiped being and Brahman, and in going beyond worship they have sought union. There have been tendencies within Buddhism to adopt a similar relation to the Buddha-principle or Buddha-nature, but when the Buddhist is clear that the Buddha-principle or nature is Emptiness-as-such, this tendency is broken. Emptiness lacks the actuality that would allow for it to be worshiped. Also, one aims not at union with Emptiness but at its realization, which is, quite simply, becoming empty or realizing that one is already empty.

The subordination of the Empty One to Emptiness is the subordination of worship to enlightenment. If for the Christian there is no such religious subordination, then there is no subordination at all. If God is the one, cosmic, everlasting actualization of ultimate reality on whom all ephemeral actualizations depend, God's nonidentity with ultimate reality in no way subordinates God to it, for God is the ultimate *actuality.* God as the ultimate actuality is just as ultimate as is Emptiness as ultimate *reality.* Emptiness is different from God, and there is no God apart from Emptiness. But it is equally true to say there is no Emptiness apart from God. Emptiness is not "above" or "beyond" God.

But is the affirmation of God as ultimate actuality compatible with the vision of Emptiness as ultimate reality? The answer must be that, to date, no formulation of the Christian understanding of God is compatible with the Buddhist vision. Yet it may be questioned whether anything essential to the Christian faith would be lost in rethinking God in Buddhist terms. The key requirement is that God be understood to be wholly, unqualifiedly empty. This would not be a new note in Christian theology, but its consistent working out would indeed be new.

God must be conceived as wholly lacking substantiality. God cannot be an agent separate or distinct from the divine activity or a patient distinguished from the divine receptivity. God must be the complete, unqualified, everlasting actualization of *pratitya-samutpada*, dependent origination. It is precisely by being perfectly empty that God, like a Buddha, is perfectly full. That is, God must be totally open to all that is and constituted by its reception.

To think of God in this way is certainly in tension with much that has been meant by the word "God" in the entire history of the West, but in time Christians might find that such a Buddhized vision of God resonates better to the revelation in Jesus than does the identification of God as being or Supreme Being.

Such a conception of God would not close the gap between Christian and Buddhist belief. The Buddhas are not gods. They have become enlightened, through eons of time. If coming back from the passing over into Buddhism meant that the Christian would believe nothing that has been absent from traditional Buddhist belief, then it would entail abandonment of most of what we have meant by God. But if it means, more reasonably, that Christians can appropriate central Buddhist insights and practices, then our results thus far are encouraging. We Christians can rethink our belief in God in light of the Buddhist insight that the ultimate reality of all things is Emptiness. Through this rethinking, our own heritage may be illumined in new ways. The result, far from being a compromise that waters down Christianity, may be a richer and purer grasp of the meaning of the God we have come to know through Jesus Christ.

Our conceptualities about God, in the very service of glorifying, have often obscured the livingness and relatedness which is the basis of our knowledge of God. To think of God as the everlasting Empty One from whom all human Emptiness is derived may help us to break out of static and repressive categories. As we think of God differently the existential meaning of that belief will also change, but it will not be reduced or weakened. At the same time, the recognition that all is empty may allow Christian theocentrism to be complemented by the profound psychological and religious benefits attained through Buddhist methods of existential realization. Theoretical acknowledgment of the complementarity of God and Emptiness may provide a context in which faith in God and realization of Emptiness can mutually fructify one another in living human experience.

IV. Pure Immanence and Partial Transcendence

I have argued that Christian faith need not involve clinging, that Christians can retain but transcend personal selfhood in a way that corresponds with the Buddhist dissolution of the personal self, and that Christians can appropriate the vision of ultimate reality as Emptiness without weakening belief in God. These are bold claims, but even if they are justified, their significance is challenged by the Buddhist call for pure immanence supported by the demonstration that all else is illusion.

A major part of the importance of personal existence is that it orients us to a larger historical context of meaning, and this cannot be left behind in the transcendence of personal existence. A major significance of belief in God is that it heightens the sense that the present here-now perspective is but one among many equally distorting and equally valid ones, all subordinated to the adequate perspective of God. If Buddhism necessarily insists that all of this represents an illusory transcendence of the here-now, then either we must reject the Buddhist analysis outright or abandon much of our Christian heritage.

To avoid this dilemma I shall argue that pure immanence in the Buddhist sense does not shut us into a single instance of dependent origination solipsistically, but rather introduces past and future into the coalescence itself. Without doubt there are values to be gained by ignoring this immanent witness to transcendence, values brilliantly expressed in the Buddhist achievement. But the analysis used to encourage detachment from past and future does not preclude the development of authentic understanding and interest in them. Such understanding is important to Christians.

Buddhism rightly points out that there is no other perspective upon the world than the here-now, and it forces recognition of the many efforts at self-deception that characterize Western thought on this point. Westerners think and speak falsely as if viewing the present from some Archimedean point without.

Nevertheless, the Buddhist formulation, while valid, is one-sided. It is true that the here-now is a coalescence of elements which are themselves here-now. But it is also true that these elements are not simply located here-now. They witness here-now to their occurrence there-then. That is, my remembered past and the star I now see in the night sky are here-now in my present experience, but I feel them here-now as temporally past and spatially distant. For here-now to be Empty is for it to allow these elements their own integrity, which includes their having-been. They are here-now as what-has-been-there-then. It is for this reason that the Buddhist can also say that in knowing oneself one who is enlightened knows all things. But if so, then the past as the having-been of elements of the here-now coalescence is not illusory. Further, the future differs from both the here-now coalescence and the there-then as the not-yet. As claim and hope it is also ingredient in the coalescence with its own distinctive integrity.

More generally, the analysis of the dependent origination of all things does not demand a doctrine of pure immanence alone.

What is immanent in this vision is by the same token transcendent, for what coalesces is not the coalescence itself but elements each with their distinctive contribution to make.

If in the here-now we attend to the *givenness* of the coalescing elements, experience each in its integrity of having-been or not-yet, we experience the here-now not as absolute, but as relative, as one among many. True, it is for us the only perspective there is, but it is free to realize itself either as one among many or in its present ultimacy. The value and validity of the Buddhist choice of the latter is not in question. But the Christian choice of the former, self-relativizing understanding is not precluded by acceptance of the Buddhist analysis. Indeed, Buddhists, too, can strike this note.

The interior witness to past and future on the part of the coalescing elements allows also for authentic memory and anticipation. Christians require this because we cannot abandon history. For us, life on this planet and especially the human experiment are unique and precious. Our understanding of what has occurred and may occur, and of the relation of the earth to the cosmos, has been deeply transformed by the scholarly study of history and by the scientific vision of nature. We orient ourselves now through Christ to the world as history, and the natural sciences enable us to understand it.

Buddhism constitutes a profound challenge to this mode of self-orientation. It correctly reminds us that there is no circumference and that therefore every point is the center. This insight shatters the naive biblical view of beginning and end as objectively given. There are no fixed parameters by which to orient ourselves. Every meaning frame by which we order our lives is our own construct. The recognition of the relativity of meaning frames to perspectives has shattering existential consequences for those who need fixed security and objective truth. But if as Christians we accpt life as an adventure, we can continue to orient ourselves even when we recognize the element of construction in the patterns we employ.

That all meaning frames are constructs does not imply that they are arbitrary or idiosyncratic. These frames are more and less illuminating, adequate, and accurate. Some are capable of being widely shared by thoughtful people, whereas others collapse quickly under examination. Some encourage generosity and openness; others inspire fear and defensiveness. Christians seek a meaning frame that provides hope without false confidence, one that takes seriously the appalling dangers of today's world while calling forth the sense of responsible freedom, and one that opens us to the contributions of such other traditions as Buddhism. Such a meaning frame does not represent the fixed circumference of all history, much less of all events, but it may be an appropriate construct from the center that is here-now.

To continue the adventure of finding meaning in history and therefore living toward the future, nevertheless expresses at an ultimate level the conviction that hope as such is not simply a construct. If there is no possibility of a future that surpasses the present in its capacity for immediacy of enjoyment, then the habit of future orientation appears irrational. The Buddhist analysis is designed to break that habit and to withdraw our energies and purposes from the future into sheer immediacy. The resulting serenity is beautiful in Christian eyes. The Christian, threatened by disillusionment with the possibilities of the future, is drawn by the Buddhist analysis to seek this serenity. But at this most precarious juncture for the whole human enterprise, such retreat from history appears to the Christian as a temptation.

There is, however, a way in which Christians can appropriate the idea of the pure immediacy of experience. It can be employed in the construction of new meaning frames as a vision of what is hoped for. The expectation of the kingdom has involved for Christians the postponement of gratification. But the kingdom is an image of a future in which such postponement is ended. The image has lost power partly because we have found it increasingly difficult to believe in a condition of fulfilled immediacy. The encounter with Nirvana provides a new way of conceiving the immediacy of blessedness for which time is no longer important.

To think of the hoped-for future in this way is not simply to postpone gratification. There is immediate gratification in working for a future in which we can believe. Furthermore, every convincing image of the future encourages an anticipatory participation in the future that is expected. In some measure the future kingdom was already realized in Jesus' ministry. If the realization of a Christianized Nirvana is the future for which we hope, we can allow ourselves now the joy of pure immersion in the moment as a part of our orientation to that future for all. In Buddhist terms, the Christian can accept the ideal of the Bodhisattva who refuses entry into Nirvana unless all sentient beings can be saved.

NOTES

1. William Johnston, *The Still Point: Reflections on Zen and Christian Mysticism* (New York: Fordham University Press, 1970), p. 187.
2. A personal communication.
3. William Johnston, *Christian Zen* (New York: Harper & Row, 1971), p. 48.
4. See Paul C. Ingram, *The Dharma of Faith: An Introduction to Classical Pure Land Buddhism* (Washington, D.C.: University Press of America, 1977). Ingram provides a concise but comprehensive history of the Pure Land school together with a useful bibliography.
5. See Alfred Bloom, *Shinran's Gospel of Pure Grace* (Tucson: University of Arizona Press, 1965). An excellent brief introduction to Shinran is found in *Letters to Shinran: A Translation of the Mattōshō*, ed. Yoshifumi Ueda (Kyoto: Hongwanji International Center, 1978). This is the first volume of a Shin Buddhism Translation Series.
6. See *The Tanni Sho: Notes Lamenting Differences*, trans. and ed. Ryusetsu Fujiwara (Kyoto: Ryukoku Translation Center, 1962), p. 60.

CHAPTER SIX

The Christian Witness to Buddhists

NEAR THE END OF THE SECOND CHAPTER two phases of movement beyond dialogue were proposed. The first is the phase of Christian self-transformation. If in the dialogue Christians have truly listened, and if in listening we have heard truth or wisdom we previously lacked, then we are called to rethink our heritage so as to incorporate that truth. When the dialogue is with representatives of other religious Ways, that truth or wisdom is rarely of the sort that can simply be added to our previous store of beliefs. If we have listened for the heart of the matter, we have heard something profound and transforming. Hence the task of rethinking is not a simple one.

Chapter Three presented the heart of the truth and wisdom of Buddhism as I have heard it from Mahayana Buddhists. It comes as a shock by its challenge not merely to secondary aspects of our Christian heritage but also to its core. It is important not to tone down the radicalness of the Buddhist intention. The radicalness is the crux of the message.

Chapter Four presented the results of some years of reflection as the first phase of the movement beyond dialogue. It is the effort to incorporate the truth and wisdom that I have heard from Buddhists and to allow it to transform Christian faith. It is an attempt to "Buddhize" Christianity, in the belief that Christ calls us today to such an effort.

The first phase was for the sake of Christianity. Christians cannot be satisfied with a Christianity that neglects or falsifies the deepest dimensions of reality. If Buddhism can teach us about this, then we should be grateful pupils. But we do not enter dialogue only for our own sake. We believe that Christ is the Truth, and that we dimly but decisively apprehend this Truth in Jesus and participate in it through him. We believe that our dialogue partners also need that Truth. We know that when we witness to this Truth without understanding the truths of our partners, our claim for its universality can hardly avoid appearing as a denial of the different truths which our partners grasp. Hence it is important, through the power of Truth, to listen and be transformed by the truths we hear before we press our case. In this way we can embody that Truth which leads to ever new truths rather than falsify it by presenting our limited truths as if they were that Truth.

But if we have embodied the Truth which we can never fully utter by being transformed by those truths which our dialogue partners offer us, then we are ready in a new way to point out to our partners their need of this Truth which we know as Christ. This does not mean that we call upon them to abandon their traditions and join the church. We have seen that many Catholic and some Protestant theologians have gone beyond this limited understanding of our mission in a pluralistic age. It does not mean that we are blind to the presence and work of Truth in our dialogue partners and in the truths and traditions they represent. But it does mean that we believe that in Jesus this Truth has been embodied in such a way that we who have been grasped by it in him have something of utmost importance to offer to those who have not incorporated him into their inner histories.

The argument in Chapter Five was that central Christian convictions can be so reformulated as to take account of what is learned from Buddhism. This implies also that the heart of Buddhist truth is not contradictory to the heart of Christian belief. In that sense it has already been shown that a Buddhist could assimilate some major Christian commitments without abandoning the central wisdom of the Buddhist tradition. But the argument was not presented in such a way as to show why Buddhists should be interested in doing this.

This chapter takes a quite different approach. It tries to show from Buddhist history that there are problems and limitations in Buddhism which point to the need for contributions which Christianity can make. Chapter Five argued that Buddhism can contribute to the fulfillment of Christianity. This chapter argues that

Christianity can contribute to the fulfillment of Buddhism. There is some overlap in the points made.

Section I makes the claim that the universalist commitment, so central to Mahayana Buddhism, has its fullest expression thus far in Pure Land Buddhism and specifically in the Jōdoshinshū denomination established by Shinran. Section II makes the case that what is named Amida in Pure Land Buddhism is what Christians call Christ. Section III shows that, if this is so, Buddhists can learn from Christians about some important characteristics of Amida to which they have not attended. The fourth section argues that Buddhism can best advance through the recognition of the decisive incarnation of Amida in the historical Jesus.

I. Buddhist Universalism

Gautama sought the salvation of all sentient beings. He did so by explaining the cause of suffering and showing the way to gain freedom from suffering. He proposed a way that did not require superhuman austerities. Nevertheless, others, including those most closely associated with him, found his path extremely difficult.

Standard Buddhist teaching in the Theravada tradition pictured the way to salvation as requiring many lifetimes. Over a period of thousands of years the rare soul could move from the ordinary human condition to that freedom from all attachment which is the life of the saint. Such a soul could then enter Nirvana.

Other Buddhists were disturbed by the elitist character of this doctrine which removed the ordinary Buddhist so far from enlightenment. They dubbed this teaching Hinayana, the lesser vehicle, and they proposed that the true Buddhist position was Mahayana, the greater vehicle. Here there is emphasis on enlightenment in this life, and hence on understanding how it can be obtained. It was in its Mahayana form that Buddhism moved into China, Korea, and Japan.

The primary interest in Mahayana has been on meditational methods which enable the meditator to realize truth. These have been highly varied, but all are quite demanding. They require time and personal discipline, and many who have tried them have still not received enlightenment.

From very early times many Buddhists felt themselves quite unable to attain enlightenment by their own efforts. They looked for help to the Buddhas. Legends grew up about Bodhisattvas, those who are spiritually ready for Buddhahood but who, out of their great compassion for the multitude, vowed not to enter Nirvana unless all sentient beings could be saved. This salvation they effected by creating worlds, called Pure Lands, to which people could go when they died. A Pure Land is not Nirvana, but unlike the present world, a Pure Land makes it easy to attain enlightenment. And whereas the requirements for attaining enlightenment in this life are still very difficult to fulfill, the requirements specified by the Bodhisattvas for entering the Pure Land on death were quite practical. They usually included the avoidance of gross immorality and calling on the name of the Buddha with sincere faith.

One such legend gained preeminence. It was said that an Indian prince by the name of Dharmakara vastly excelled all the others, creating a Pure Land which subsumed them all and simplifying the requirements for entering it to the greatest extent possible. This prince then became the Buddha Amida. For the Pure Land tradition it is Amida who is the true savior.

The general Buddhist understanding in China was that the primary and most appropriate way in which one should seek salvation was through the monastic life with its meditational disciplines. But for those who could not or would not submit to this pattern of life, a second, lower, possibility was acknowledged. It was this to which many ordinary lay people turned as their only hope. Hence the Pure Land tradition in Mahayana Buddhism was important as the expression of its concern for the universality of salvation.

In Japan in the twelfth century, two developments occurred. First Hōnen and his disciples came to the conclusion that although in past epochs self-salvation through discipline had been possible, in this evil time it is not. The merciful vow of Amida, far from providing an inferior alternative to the superior self-salvation, offered the only possible way of salvation. And second, especially in the formulations of Shinran, faith was declared to be the *only* requirement for receiving the grace through which alone salvation was possible, and this faith as well was understood to be the gift of Amida. In Section I of the previous chapter Shinran was compared with Luther in this regard. With great insight Shinran understood that if salvation is for all it may not depend on any human merit but solely on the grace of Amida.

Whereas Shinran was correct that the universal compassion of Buddhism could best come to expression through his doctrine of salvation by grace through faith alone, he was not inclusive in other respects. In this, too, he resembled Luther. When Luther understood that monastic disciplines were irrelevant to justification, he opposed monasteries. Similarly Hōnen and Shinran opposed the disciplines and meditational practices of other Buddhist schools.

But this exclusiveness is not necessary. Christians today know that although they are justified apart from special spiritual disciplines, they are free to practice those disciplines. The disciplines they are free to practice include Buddhist as well as traditional ones. They practice them not in order to be justified but because they want the depth and spiritual maturity that such disciplines can help to provide. There is nothing in Pure Land Buddhism to prevent its encouragement of the important and effective disciplines developed in other schools such as Zen. What is important is that salvation not be understood in such a way that people are *driven* into these disciplines. The Pure Land Buddhist or the Christian is free to practice Zen meditation or not to practice it. There is no obligation. Understood in this way, Pure Land thought and practice can rightly see themselves as the fulfillment of the Buddhist quest for universality.[1]

II. Amida as Christ

Christians sometimes use "Christ" as a proper name for Jesus. This is misleading. At the very least it should be distinguished as a title given to Jesus because of his redemptive work. The Christian knows Jesus *as* the Christ. Similarly it is possible to use "Amida" as a proper name for the Indian prince Dharmakara, but this too is misleading. It is only as this human being became a Buddha that he acquired the name Amida. There is some parallelism here, but it is far from perfect, and in this usage "Christ" and "Amida" do not refer to the same reality. Amida is not Christ in this sense.

But the meanings of Amida and Christ have not remained at this level. Christ could be thought of as the preexistent one who took on human form in Jesus and then returned to the right hand of the Father, with or without his human body. Amida is the Buddha who is now in Nirvana. Both Christ and Amida are divine beings, but they are quite different. This Christ is a supernatural being subordinate to God and most naturally conceived along Arian lines. Amida is one Buddha among others, however great. There are similarities, but this Christ is not Amida and this Amida is not Christ.

The early church, however, repudiated Arian subordinationism. Christ is not a creature, however exalted. Christ is God. But when we say Christ, we are not simply referring to God in general but speaking of God as everlasting Word, creatively and redemptively working in the world. This is the Truth which opens us to all truths. Similarly, in Pure Land Buddhist reflection, Amida did not remain one Buddha among others. Amida came to name instead the reality which is incarnate in all Buddhas. This raises the question whether Amida as that which is incarnate in all Buddhas and Christ as the creative and redemptive activity of God in the world name the same reality. I believe they do, but this must be shown.

When pressed along the lines indicated, Pure Land teaching can lose much of its distinctiveness. What is incarnate in all Buddhas, it is generally understood, is Emptiness or Nirvana. Amida can then become another name for Emptiness without altering the meaning of Emptiness. If this path is followed, then again Amida is not Christ.

Nevertheless, there is an important distinction which preserves Pure Land's distinctive teaching. It can best be made in relation to the traditional Buddhist teaching about the Buddha body. In this teaching ultimate reality, understood as that which is embodied by each Buddha, is called the Body of Dharma or *Dharmakaya.* The form taken by *Dharmakaya* in individual human beings when they become Buddhas is the Manifest Body or *Nirmanakaya.* The form taken by *Dharmakaya* in the Buddhas who rule over their Pure Lands is the Body of Bliss or *Sambhogakaya.* Amida is not the *Dharmakaya* as such but rather the *Sambhogakaya.*

The true character of the *Sambhogakaya* is manifest in the vows of the Bodhisattvas and especially in the vow of Dharmakara. But in the deepest understanding, Amida is not simply the new and glorified form of Dharmakara as he rules over his Pure Land. Amida is the *Sambhogakaya* itself which is perfectly embodied or incarnate in the vow of Dharmakara. What is there manifest is wisdom and compassion, the essential characteristics of the *Sambhogakaya.*

In most schools of Buddhist thought, even when Amida is understood in this way, he is subordinate to the *Dharmakaya.* This is because the *Dharmakaya,* ultimate reality as such, is beyond and above the other manifestations of the Buddha body. Amida as the *Sambhogakaya* still has a distinct character, the character of wisdom and compassion. The *Dharmakaya* as such is beyond all forms. Ultimate reality assumes the form of *Sambhogakaya* for the sake of those who cannot realize ultimate reality as such, but this is a concession to human weakness and should not be taken as the ultimate truth. In this view, the deepest and purest achievement of enlightenment can bypass the *Sambhogakaya* and realize the *Dharmakaya* itself.

Even among Jōdoshinshū believers this relativization of Amida and his subordination to the *Dharmakaya* is sometimes accepted. This is easy for Christians to understand because similar tendencies were present in the early church where the Logos was often regarded as subordinate to the Father and sometimes even as a creature. But Christians recognized that faith in Christ can be existentially ultimate only if Christ is truly God. Insofar as anything else is regarded as superior to Amida, Amida cannot name for Buddhists what Christ names for Christians.

The conceptual and traditional pressure on Pure Land Buddhists to acknowledge the subordination of Amida to the *Dharma-*

kaya is greater than the analogous pressure on Christians to subordinate Christ to the Father. But in Shinran himself this pressure is strongly resisted, at least so far as religion is concerned. In our concrete situation, Amida is ultimate. Amida is ultimate reality *for us*, because ultimate reality for us *is* wise and compassionate.

Here as elsewhere, I have found the conceptuality of Alfred North Whitehead useful in the understanding of Buddhism. In Chapters Four and Five I followed the Western tradition in calling ultimate reality *esse*, being, or *Sein*. Whitehead's term is creativity. He, too, recognizes that ultimate reality as creativity is beyond all forms since in principle it is susceptible of any form whatever. In many respects his analysis of creativity corresponds to some Buddhist accounts of the *Dharmakaya*, especially as *Dharmakaya* is explained in terms of dependent origination.

But Whitehead believes that in actuality, although creativity is completely without any character of its own, it is never experienced apart from a primordial ordering of the infinite array of the forms or pure possibilities. This ordering is directed to the realization of novel intensities of feeling in the actual instances of creativity, that is, in such creatures as ourselves. Thus what is wholly without character in itself has been primordially characterized by a decision that ordered what is possible for the sake of all creatures. Whitehead calls this character of creativity the Primordial Nature of God.[2] There is no creativity not characterized by this Nature.

Pure Land Buddhism has come to its formulations in quite a different way, but they are remarkably congruous with Whitehead's. In Amida the *Dharmakaya* has a primordial character. This character is fully revealed in the vow of Dharmakara as the aim to save all sentient beings. There is for Shinran no access to an ultimate reality that is not characterized by this primal vow.

Viewed in this way, the tendency to subordinate ultimate reality as primordially characterized to ultimate reality apart from any character appears arbitrary. All that could ever be *actually* experienced or realized is ultimate reality *with* its primordial character. To regard ultimate reality in abstraction from this character as superior to ultimate reality as thus characterized seems to express an unnecessary prejudice.

There are at least two Buddhist reasons for opposing the view I am presenting. The first is that we can have no advance notion of enlightenment, even that it will realize wisdom and compassion. To assert that enlightenment will be characterized in this way implies some preestablished pattern to which it must conform. This is precisely the way of thinking which must be abandoned if enlightenment is to be attained.

However, this objection does not apply in relation to Whitehead's understanding. The primordial ordering of forms for the sake of promoting intensities in the creatures does not make possible prediction of what specific forms will be relevant. On the contrary, it is precisely this ordering that is the basis for creative novelty and appropriate spontaneity in the world. That the act performed by the Enlightened One expresses wise compassion may be recognized when it is performed, but the anticipation that the act will be one of wise compassion does not afford any way of predicting its particular form. Wise compassion is always spontaneous.

A second Buddhist reason for opposing this view is the claim that people can realize the *Dharmakaya* as such apart from all forms. But this claim is not evidently established by history or present experience. All Buddhists expect that Buddhas will be wise and compassionate. In standard Buddhist teaching this wisdom and compassion express their full realization of ultimate reality. There is no apparent evidence of a higher state in which wisdom and compassion are left behind. Hence it is not clear how this attainment can be used to argue for the superiority of the *Dharmakaya* as such to the *Dharmakaya* as characterized by wisdom and compassion, that is, to the *Sambhogakaya* or Amida.

It is sometimes held that the teaching of the wisdom and compassion of ultimate reality as *Sambhogakaya* is *upaya*, that is, skillful means for drawing people toward the realization of an ultimate reality that has no character whatsoever. But is it not equally possible that the teaching that ultimate reality can be realized apart from any character whatsoever is skillful means for encouraging the withdrawal of attention from all forms, including the most attractive ones? It may well be that in order to realize ultimate reality with its wisdom and compassion through Zen discipline, for example, one must detach oneself completely from any concern about wisdom and compassion. But this provides no support for any ultimate subordination of Amida to the *Dharmakaya* as such.

Whitehead's account of the Primordial Nature of God addresses the same feature of reality as that spoken of by Shinran as the primal vow of Amida. Both of these are remarkably analogous to the Johannine and patristic accounts of the Word of God or Logos or Truth which is Christ. That, too, is a primordial character apart from which nothing exists. It is a creative-redemptive character.

The conclusion from the above is that Amida is Christ. That is, the feature of the totality of reality to which Pure Land Buddhists refer when they speak of Amida is the same as that to which Christians refer when we speak of Christ. This does not mean that Buddhists are completely accurate in their account of this reality—nor that Christians are. It does mean that Christians can gain further knowledge about Christ by studying what Buddhists have learned about Amida. It means also that Buddhists can gain further knowledge about Amida by studying what Christians have learned about Christ. Indeed, we should be able to reflect together about many questions of concern to both of us. But truly joint work is still in our future. For the present we consider in partial separation what each can learn from the other.

III. What Buddhists Can Learn from Christians

The preceding has dealt in general terms with what Christians can appropriate from Buddhism and included some discussion for the specific contribution of Pure Land Buddhists. For example, Christians can learn that Christ's concern is for all sentient creatures and not for human beings alone. Also we can more clearly perceive that much of what we have regarded until now as faith in Christ is idolatrous. That is, Christ is too often understood as a feature of reality bound to particular times and places and yet is treated as absolute. Such faith is a form of clinging from which reflection about Amida can help to set us free. It correlates with Arian heresy rather than Christian orthodoxy. Christ is God and not anything more limited.

Even when it is recognized that Christ is God, faith in Christ can still be a kind of clinging. One may cling to some past manifestation of Christ or identify faith in Christ with particular beliefs and practices. Against this the church at its best has taught that Christ is Truth itself and not a particular truth. To have faith in Christ is to be open to all truth and to all reality—not to cling to one truth and one reality. To trust Christ is to abandon all prejudice, all defenses, and to receive all that can be received. The recognition that Christ is Amida will help us toward this faith.

But in this section our interest is primarily in what Buddhists can learn of Amida when they recognize that Amida is Christ. Two areas of investigation are potentially fruitful here: 1. The sense in which Amida is personal, and 2. The sense in which Amida is ethical.

1. The view of Amida as ultimate reality characterized by wisdom and compassion is the most fully demythologized form of the understanding of Amida. But in this form Amida is somewhat less personal than is Christ in the dominant forms of Christian thought. Since the question of the sense in which God is personal is important, we will consider somewhat further the relation of Christian thinking about Christ to Shinran's understanding of Amida.

From one point of view the personal element is just as strong in the teaching concerning Amida as in the idea of the Christian God. Amida is Dharmakara, a legendary human being who has become a Buddha. As *a* Buddha he certainly retains personal characteristics even though he is now radically trans-human. But since this suggests that Amida is simply one Buddha among others, I did not emphasize this approach above when arguing that Amida is recognizable as Christ or the Word of God.

Still, we can see in Pure Land Buddhism, as in Christianity, the effort to hold together the universal and the personal in that to which faith is directed. Amida is that Buddha in whom the intentions of all Buddhas are fulfilled. In a sense Amida includes all other Buddhas without ceasing to be a personal being. As the Body of Bliss or *Sambhogakaya* assumed by Dharmakara, he is also the *Sambhogakaya* as such.

The point here is not to suggest that Pure Land Buddhism has solved the problem of holding together the personal and the universal elements in the understanding of Amida. The point is only that, as in Christianity, both elements are present and prized. To whatever extent Christian theology has succeeded in attaining a doctrine of God that does justice to both elements in a coherent manner, this can be of help to Pure Land Buddhism, too.

There is another sense of the personal, however, which is important for many Christians but runs counter to the mainstream of Pure Land teaching. This is the element of interaction between God and human beings. Christian prayer is ordinarily experienced as presupposing that God "hears" us. That means that God takes account of contingent human acts as they occur. Biblical language suggests that God rejoices when a sinner repents and knows when even a sparrow dies. What we do to the least of our brothers and sisters we do also to Christ. It even seems that God's activity is adjusted to changing circumstances.

This imagery has been in tension with that orthodox philosophical theology which has insisted upon divine immutability. The implications of this doctrine are that while God acts upon us, we can in no way affect God's experience. God's action expresses perfect love, but this is a purely active love, not one of receptivity or empathy. In the twentieth century there has been extensive theological critique of this understanding of divine immutability. There has been an effort to give less qualified affirmation to the biblical imagery of personal interaction between God and human beings. Philosophical theologians influenced by Whitehead have long argued against the monopolar prejudice of traditional theism in favor of a dipolarity of activity and receptivity in God.

Whitehead's formulation of this dipolarity is in terms of the Primordial and the Consequent Natures of God. It is the Primordial Nature which qualifies creativity in a way so strikingly similar to the qualification of the *Dharmakaya* by the primal vow. Just as the Primordial Nature of God is the primordial decision for the sake of all creatures, even more clearly the primal vow is made for the sake of all sentient beings. But there is no sense among Buddhists that we can contribute anything to Amida. There is no encouragement of prayers of petition or intercession, no idea that Amida "hears" our prayers. There is, in other words, nothing comparable to what Whitehead calls the Consequent Nature of God.

Much of traditional Christian theology also lacks this element, but in actual Christian piety, based on biblical imagery and Christian experience, the sense of personal interaction with God has been so strong that it is worth considering whether Buddhists can extend their understanding of Amida to include this aspect of what Christians have found in Christ.

For many Buddhists there is a sharp contrast between Samsara as the world of dependent origination *(pratitya-samutpada* or *engi)* and Nirvana as the perfect world of the enlightened. Given such a contrast there would be strong reason to deny that the Enlightened One could be affected by events in the world of *pratitya-samutpada*. The Enlightened One might exert a gracious influence in this sphere, but there could be no reciprocal effect.

However, Nagarjuna, and much of Mahayana Buddhism following him, rejected this idea of two worlds. There is no world beyond the world of *pratitya-samutpada*. It is in the true realization of *that* world that enlightenment lies. In this case the Buddhas are not outside this world; they are the perfect realization of this world. That means that they are perfectly affected by everything we do at the same time that we are affected by them. The Buddha unites perfect receptivity to perfect activity.

What now of the *Sambhogakaya* which is incarnated in each Buddha? Should it not have the same duality of relations? At least in Christian experience and teaching it has seemed appropriate to believe that the One that gives gracious character to ultimate reality also responds perfectly to all that happens in the world. It is hard to see that anything of worth would be lost to Buddhists if they assimilated from the Christian knowledge of Christ the conviction that our lives are in this way of importance to Amida.

2. What Christians most miss in Buddhism is often referred to as the ethical and especially the social-ethical emphasis. Some Buddhists have acknowledged that in this area they have something to learn from Christianity. And there are already movements among Japanese Buddhists seeking to fill this lacuna. Especially in the area of activity for peace have Buddhists given leadership.

Nevertheless, the basic difference between Christians and Buddhists remains quite marked. The difficulty is in stating this accurately and fairly, for sweeping statements to the effect that Buddhism is not an ethical religion or lacks a social ethic can be extremely misleading. It is well, first, to state what is *not* lacking.

The point is not that Buddhist cultures fail to do a good job of socialization. They have well-developed structures of society with clear understanding of socially desirable behavior patterns, and their members conform to social needs and expectations with a minimum of coercion. On the whole, Buddhist societies probably function better than Christian ones, and could well be said to be more moral.

Secondly, Buddhism tends to make the mores of a society more humane. It discourages violence and greed. It works against exploitation of the weak. Its opposition to the caste system in India reflects this basic humanism. Buddhist societies have also, on the whole, been more pacific than Christian ones. One would not expect wars to be fought for the sake of Buddha as Christians have fought for the sake of Christ. Buddhist societies tend to be more tolerant religiously.

Third, there is no lack of personal kindness and generosity in Buddhist societies. Buddhism encourages these virtues as much as Christianity and perhaps inhibits them less. They are directly related to the quest for enlightenment and especially to its attainment. They may even be expressed in heroic ways. Buddhists are as likely as Christians to sacrifice themselves for the good of the community.

Fourth, Buddhists shoulder their responsibilities within the community with as much fortitude and discipline as do Christians. Buddhism encourages its adherents to work faithfully and diligently at the assigned tasks, not seeking recognition or reward. In this respect also the level of morality in Buddhist societies is high.

What seems to the Christian to be missing, then, is not virtue or goodness. What is lacking is a trans-social norm by virtue of which society is judged. Even this must be stated with care. Buddhist humanism does provide a check against the tendency to value people only in terms of their social role or relationship to others. Human beings do count as such, and hence their welfare does stand as a norm against existing social structure and behavior. But this potential principle of leverage is rarely thematically developed. On the whole, Buddhism does not encourage attention by its adherents to critical evaluation of social and political programs or exhort them to be in the forefront of movements of social protest. This seems to be because the mode of the relation of individuals to trans-social reality, namely, to Emptiness or to Amida, does not direct them to a judgment of social structures and their historical roles.

Initially at least, these comments should be taken as descriptive rather than as negative criticism. Christians are deeply divided as to whether the socially critical aspect of our heritage is of central importance or whether our faith, like Buddhism, relates primarily to our inwardness. Some converts to Buddhism find its freedom from this struggle and from the guilt associated with it profoundly attractive and satisfying. Buddhists may point to the extremely ambiguous effects of Christian efforts to shape history and argue that the results for all will be better if those efforts are abandoned.

But from the Christian point of view, this lack *is* a flaw. Many Christians look at the global situation historically and are appalled by the danger that human beings may bring upon themselves—unparalleled disaster and suffering if not actual extinction. Even if the human race muddles through these threats, we find intolerable the level of suffering inflicted on the world's poor and on our fellow nonhuman creatures through wrongly conceived programs of so-called "development." It seems of utmost importance that humane people guide in re-directing us away from our destructive political course. Any form of Christianity or of Buddhism which turns the attention and energy of humane people away from these global problems is inadequate.

The question, then, is whether Buddhists could discover from the Christian experience of Christ those aspects of Amida which would strengthen their critical orientation to the socio-historical world. That question can be approached through consideration of the characteristics of biblical and Western ethics which have functioned in this way.

In the Bible God is often conceived as lawgiver and judge. Although Jewish society in part embodies these laws and is thereby sanctioned by this view of God, God's commands are frequently experienced as judging the society. Certainly God stands beyond society as a trans-social source of norms whose commands have direct social relevance. The question as to whether society is functioning rightly is constantly renewed.

There is no doubt that this biblical view directs attention to issues of social justice, but it has its own problems. First, it has a strongly mythological cast, which can lead to the attribution to God of almost any command. Second, it produces a legalistic structure of life and self-understanding, against which Christianity is constantly struggling and which has driven many of its most sensitive children from its fold. Thirdly, it can work against the growth of creative imagination and sensitivity, which are so badly needed if problems are to be dealt with wisely.

The first can be removed by going from a mythological deity to categorical imperatives, which can be worked out in a fully rational system. But this does little to overcome the other objections. Living by categorical imperatives is even more legalistic than living in obedience to divine commands. The fact that the source of one's principles is one's own reason adds arrogance to the problematic. And these principles are likely to interfere with intelligent responsiveness to the actual needs of people and institutions.

Even if Christians could endorse the theory of divine commands or categorical imperatives, we could not recommend them as a possible development of Buddhist thought. Buddhism offers a way to escape from the too-structured world into freedom and spontaneity. To propose that it adopt legalism as part of its goal would be too ad hoc and distasteful to be relevant at all.

The Bible offers other images of God's relation to the world more appropriate to Christ. Deeper than the image of the one who commands is that of the one who offers and calls. This image is in greater continuity with that of Amida and yet extends it in the direction that seems important to me.

The call of Christ can be understood as mythically as the command of God. But it can be demythologized without reducing the actual role of Christ. The call consists in introducing into our existence, moment by moment, possibilities for our self-actualization that lead to good for ourselves and for others. These involve a tension between what simply is and what might be and should be. They involve some urge or impulse to the realization of desirable possibilities. By doing so they introduce a space for human freedom. We are free to create ourselves in relation both to the actual world from which we come and to these new possibilities for our existence. The effective working of these liberating and challenging possibilities is the presence of the creative and redemptive Christ. Christ is present as the life-giving call to be more than we have been both for our own sake and for the sake of others.

The relation between traditional Buddhism and Christianity can be clarified by attention again to *pratitya-samutpada*, dependent origination. This is the coalescence of the world into the new experience. That world includes both what is actual and what is possible. Christian spirituality has concentrated on discerning the possibilities, determining which constitute God's call, and responding appropriately thereto. Buddhist disciplines have concentrated on the realization that what is occurring is just this coalescence in which there is finally no dualism of subject and object. Attention has been directed to the actual world as it coalesces rather than to novel possibilities.

Buddhist disciplines have been far more refined and effective than Christian ones, partly because the latter have not overcome the illusions of substance and dualism. Further, the openness attained by the Buddhist is in fact an openness to the possibilities of each situation as well as to the actualities that constitute it. But because Buddhism does not encourage attention to this side of the coalescence and does not thematize what is involved, the Christian misses in Buddhism the ethics which arise from the core experience of Christ.

For the Pure Land Buddhist who recognizes that Amida is Christ it may be possible to expand the understanding and experience of Amida's grace. Amida's vow may be understood to give us freedom, to invite us quite specifically to achieve what can be achieved by freedom in each moment, and to make possible the response to that invitation. To extend the understanding of Amida in that way need not violate what the Buddhist has come to know of Amida in the past.

If the call of Amida is to be understood as more than immediate and private, if it is to be experienced as having social and world-historical meaning, then other changes in traditional Buddhism will also be needed. Buddhism has concentrated on liberating us from our false conceptualizations. These include the ways in which we understand society and history, and ourselves as participants in these. We are sorely in need of such liberation. But this freedom should be used to arrive at better concepts and theories. If we are called to live for others as well as for ourselves, we are also called to think in such a way that our decisions will truly benefit others rather than worsen their lot. Pure spontaneity works well in immediate human relations, but it is a poor basis for public policy. Yet that policy will be immensely benefited if those who have freed themselves from the illusion of a substantial self and from the attachments that go with that illusion can help to correct the illusions which are so deeply built into our social and economic theories. A Christianized Buddhism has much to contribute.

IV. The Centrality of Christ

It is not uncommon for Christians to recognize that outside of explicit Christian faith, people can in some way know and trust Christ. Indeed, the development of the Logos doctrine in the early church was partly for the sake of understanding how wise and virtuous pagans were oriented in their lives to the same truth as that which Christians know in Jesus. Hence to use the same doctrine today to show that some Buddhists also put their faith in the one Logos which Christians know as incarnate in Jesus is simply to continue an ancient Christian tradition.

But Christians also recognize the incarnation of that Logos in a particular historical figures, Jesus of Nazareth. Is there any reason internal to Buddhism to affirm this Christian teaching about Jesus? In particular, are there inner characteristics of Jōdoshinshū which impel it, precisely for the sake of its own adequate development, to appropriate biblical history and the centrality of Jesus within that history? Clearly this would be a major development in the history of religions, but the shifts involved would be no greater than those proposed for Christianity in the preceding chapter. Let us consider how such a development might come about.

Internal to Jōdoshinshū teaching are certain tensions. Shinran did not ask people to put their total faith in Amida on his own authority or on the basis of clear empirical evidence of Amida's graciousness. He called for faith on the basis of what was presented in the tradition as an event in the remote past—the vow of an Indian prince, Dharmakara, and his creation of a Pure Land. Shinran presupposed the general Buddhist confidence that a Bodhisattva had the ability and the compassion to act in this way for the salvation of others. Much of the effectiveness of Pure Land teaching has been derived from the power of this story to evoke grateful belief and to convince the hearer of the reality of the Pure Land.

Until recently Japanese Buddhists have felt little compulsion to discriminate historical fact from legends and myths. The point of all stories was to lead to present realization of truth rather than to provide factual information about past occurrences. The story of Dharmakara could provide confidence in the salvific power of the vow without raising clearly focused questions about historical factuality. This is still true for many Buddhists.

Today, however, historical consciousness and critical historical methods increasingly characterize the mentality of thoughtful Japanese. The question of truth and falsity does arise with respect to traditional Buddhist stories as it does in the West with respect to biblical stories. When this happens, Gautama appears as a historical person, and efforts can be made to distinguish his original teaching from latter attributions. But Dharmakara can only be seen as a mythical figure.

Pure Land Buddhists have several options. They may insist that a mythical story is just as good as a historical one since the point is the encouragement of present faith. When this option is chosen, belief in the gracious character of ultimate reality loses its grounding in such other Buddhist doctrines as the saving power of the vow of a Boddhisattva. One may continue to argue that the believing state of mind associated with the repetition of Amida's name is an effective way of attaining enlightenment here and now, and such an assertion may or may not be true. This is a different religious world from that of salvation by grace through faith.

A second option is to take the authority of the historical Gautama as the basis of confidence in the Other Power. The Dharmakara story can then be seen as a way of emphasizing essential features of Gautama's own teaching. But this proves difficult to sustain in the light of historical research.

A third option is to direct trust to Shinran himself. This is probably the most common response among the followers of Jōdoshinshū. It is before the statue of Shinran that they kneel most often, and it is his teachings to which they are most likely to listen in confidence. In him they find a clearly historical ground for their faith.

Nevertheless, this option, too, has its problems. Whereas the authority of a Zen master may be his own experience, Shinran did not present himself in this way. He pointed away from himself to that Other Power in which he placed his faith on the basis of authoritative tradition. To take Shinran seriously from an historical point of view, one must examine the validity of the tradition to which he appeals and the accuracy of his interpretation. Such a critical historical investigation is bound to raise problems for believers.

Consider the matter in general terms. Belief in the graciousness of reality is bound up with beliefs about the actual course of events. Equally, beliefs about the actual course of events are bound up with beliefs about reality. In the Pure Land traditions, belief about reality may play the primary role, whereas in Christianity beliefs about the actual course of events may be primary. But in both cases we deal with a circle in which both aspects are needed. Both circles center in the graciousness that characterizes ultimate reality, and both have depended for their convincing power on recounting stories believed to be true.

Two hundred years ago, the Christian account of events had become highly doubtful. As it lost its convincing power, the beliefs about God and the world that were associated with it also eroded. Christians fought back in various ways. One of the most important was by leading the effort to replace the mythical history we had been telling by an historically accurate one. That task will never be finished, but it has gone far enough now that little doubt remains that there *is* an historical story to tell and that its deepest meaning can be understood as just as supportive of belief in the graciousness of God as the mythical story could ever have been.

The new story relates to the totality of world history in new ways. What is learned from this story can illumine and be illumined by the entirety of the natural-historical processes that have brought us to where we now are. As Christianity more and more fully extricates itself from its mythical and parochial past and comes to live out of the inclusive history to which it can give meaning and direction, its long period of decline may come to an end. In that inclusive history the history of Buddhism must play an important role. In the preceding chapter I indicated some of the deep changes still needed if Christianity in this way is to become a universal faith.

Jōdoshinshū has not yet worked through the crisis of the relation of history to faith. If this crisis must be faced, then in some respects its problems are more acute even than those faced by Christianity, for its basis is still further removed from the actual course of history. It can indeed find in Gautama himself and in the history of Buddhism much to support it, but its most distinctive teaching is the one that is least adequately supported in this tradition prior to Shinran himself. However, there is nothing about

Buddhist self-understanding that leads to the necessity of finding the requisite history solely in India and East Asia. On the contrary, Buddhism intends universality. It, too, needs an inclusive view of all things, and today such a view must include world history. World history includes the history of Israel and the event of Jesus. The history that supports the Christian understanding of the graciousness of God supports equally the Jōdoshinshū understanding of the wisdom and compassion that characterize ultimate reality. It provides also the grounds for a desirable expansion of the Pure Land Buddhist understanding of Amida.

Until the attitude of mutual suspicion and defensiveness between Christians and Buddhists is fully overcome, it is inconceivable that Jōdoshinshū would appeal heavily to Christian history for its support. But once that attitude is truly superseded, there is no reason in principle why Buddhists cannot internalize the Palestinian as well as the Indian past. It is in Palestine, rather than in India, that history, when it is read as centering in Jesus, provides the strongest basis for believing that we are saved by grace through faith.

V. Conclusion

The first two chapters of this book described the road to dialogue and the present ferment of reflection about the meaning of dialogue for Christians. In the latter part of Chapter Two I argued that authentic dialogue must lead beyond dialogue to the radical transformation of the dialogue partners. Christians must first cross over, genuinely and deeply exposing ourselves to the wisdom of the other. Then we must come back, facing the task of restructuring our heritage in the light of what we have learned. Chapters Four and Five illustrated this process in relation to Mahayana Buddhism.

It is also my conviction that Christians have an additional responsibility. We not only need to be open to truth wherever we can find it and engage in the hard work of incorporating it into our theology, we also need to witness to the truth with which we have been entrusted through our own history. We know that too often in the past we have confused accidental cultural accretions with that truth and have idolatrously identified that truth with our own opinions. We also know that we have usually spoken without listening. For all of this we must repent. But to repent of past mistakes does not entail abandoning our witness. It means learning to witness aright. And the goal of that witness is to lead the other to attend to what we believe to be truth and to be transformed by it.

That is evangelism, the announcement as we understand it of the gospel of Jesus Christ. That is not the recitation of set formulae. Such are too often experienced as bad news by the hearer, who feels badgered and beaten by them, forced to accept or reject ambiguous claims without the refinement and development they need. Our word is good news only if it reveals possibilities which are truly positive ones for the hearers. We cannot engage in true evangelism today except as we first listen and learn and transform ourselves in light of what we have learned. But when we have been attentive to the ambiguities in the situation of others, when we have been transformed by the truth they can teach us, then it is also time to try to show them how faith in Jesus Christ can creatively transform their traditions in such a way as to free them from bondage. This chapter has illustrated what this kind of evangelism might be in relation to some segments of Mahayana Buddhism.

Our question now is how such a transformed Buddhism would be related to the transformed Christianity proposed in the preceding chapter. Clearly these will be far closer than any now existing forms of Christianity and Buddhism. Yet there would continue to be differences rooted in the profoundly different roads they have traveled. To what extent these differences would disappear as each appropriated more fully the history and truth of the other, only time can tell. It is not clear that this would matter very much. From the Christian point of view, if Buddhists realize the rich meaning of faith in Jesus Christ, there is no reason to hope that they would also become like us in those many ways that are determined by our dominantly Western historical experience. Why should they become Roman Catholics, Southern Baptists, Missouri

Synod Lutherans, members of the United Church of Christ in Japan or join the nonchurch Christian movement there? Similarly, if Christians can realize the truth of the Buddhist doctrine of Nirvana, no essential Buddhist concern is served by the Easternization of Christianity in ways that are only accidentally related to that realization. A Buddhized Christianity and a Christianized Buddhism may continue to enrich each other and human culture generally through their differences.

This vision clearly has implications for the Christian mission. I suggest that in relation to other religious Ways today this has two main features neither of which has been prominent in missiology in the past. First, it is the mission of Christianity to *become* a universal faith in the sense of taking into itself the alien truths that others have realized. This is no mere matter of addition. It is instead a matter of creative transformation. An untransformed Christianity, that is, a Christianity limited to its own parochial traditions, cannot fulfill its mission of realizing the universal meaning of Jesus Christ. It can only continue to offer its fragment alongside the offerings of other traditions. When it appeals for total commitment to so fragmentary a realization of Christ, it is idolatrous. When, to avoid idolatry, it asks for only fragmentary commitment to the fragment of truth it offers, it ceases to express the ultimacy of the claim of Christ and continues its inevitable decay. Only as, in faithfulness to Christ, it opens itself to transformation can it ask people to participate wholeheartedly. Thus the most pressing Christian mission is the mission of self-transformation.

Second, it is the mission of a self-transforming Christianity to invite other religious traditions to undergo self-transformation as well. There is nothing wrong with opening our doors to individual converts from other traditions. Indeed, if we begin seriously to undergo self-transformation we will need the help of those who have known other truths from within other traditions. But more important than the conversion of individual Buddhists, Hindus, or Muslims is the conversion of Buddhism, Hinduism, and Islam. I have tried to indicate what that might mean in the case of Mahayana Buddhism. Equally concrete descriptions are possible in other cases. Our mission is to display the universal meaning of Christ freed from our past compulsion to contradict the truths known in other traditions. As long as we present Christ as the opponent of something that others know to be true, they will not be open to hearing what Christ has to say to them. But once we allow Christ to speak apart from the impediments we have placed in the way, Christ will carry out the authentic Christian mission. Christ as Truth will transform the truths of all other traditions even as they transform ours.

NOTES

1. This, of course, is a claim made by some Jōdoshinshū Buddhists, for example, by Prof. Yoshifumi Ueda.

2. "The primordial nature of God is the acquirement by creativity of a primordial character." Alfred North Whitehead, *Process and Reality*, corrected edition, eds. David Ray Griffin and Donald W. Sherburne, (New York: Free Press, 1978), p. 344.

Buddhism, Christianity, and the Philosophy of Whitehead

I HAVE LONG BELIEVED that Whitehead's conceptuality is fruitful both for the formulation of Christian theology and for the understanding and interpretation of Buddhist thought.[1] The material in this book is my first sustained effort to display this fruitfulness with respect to Buddhism. Critics who have not denied a certain success have raised two questions to which I wish to reply briefly in this postscript.

First, whereas I argue for the importance of learning from the other tradition what is new to one's own, have I not in fact simply appropriated from Buddhism what I have already learned from Whitehead? Am I not inviting other Christians to adopt the Whiteheadian philosophy in the guise of asking them to learn from Buddhism?

This is a difficult question to answer fairly. The suspicion is partly warranted. The truth of Buddhism which I invite other Christians to accept does not require me to renounce Whitehead's philosophy, whereas I do believe it requires Christians to break in a radical way from substantialist and dualist philosophical commitments. I am implicitly arguing that adoption of Whitehead's conceptuality will assist Christians in understanding and learning from Buddhism, and I have not clearly shown that those who have already adopted Whitehead's way of thinking have something new to learn.

Nevertheless, as a Whiteheadian I have found myself changed in my encounter with Buddhism. Although Whitehead offers a remarkably helpful bridge toward understanding Buddhism, neither he nor most of us influenced by him have crossed that bridge or taken full advantage of the possibilities he affords. My encounter with Buddhism has shown me how we Whiteheadians have consistently interpreted Whitehead in a way that reduces his radical break with substantialist and dualist modes of thought and how Whitehead himself was not able fully to carry through his own intentions against the pull of the language which he could not avoid using. If I should write a summary of Whitehead's thought today, it would be quite different from what I wrote fifteen years ago and from the other secondary literature as well. My new summary might make Whitehead more difficult for Westerners to accept.

Whitehead distinguishes two modes of process which he calls transition and concrescence. In studying Buddhist writers I came to the conclusion that what some of them described as *pratitya-samutpada* was what Whitehead called concrescence. This provided me with a bridge for understanding, but it did not give me an already established understanding. The detailed analysis of concrescence to be found in Whitehead was quite irrelevant to what the Buddhists were saying, and yet this had absorbed almost all the interest of Whitehead and his followers. The Buddhist point was to realize that at any given time what one is is nothing but such a concrescence. There is no suggestion that Whitehead ever stressed this point or encouraged his readers to think that such realization would be salvific. His conceptuality allows one to see that this might be so. It did not on its own actually suggest this possibility to him or to those influenced by him. I, at least, learned this only from Buddhists. I believe that I have yet much more to learn from them about this most fundamental reality, much that would have been new and surprising to Whitehead as well. My claim for the usefulness of Whitehead is not, therefore, that his philosophy already contains the truth of Buddhism. It does not. My claim is that it enables us to learn what Buddhists have to teach without surrendering the truth that our own Christian tradition bequeaths us.

The second critical question is whether I am claiming that the usefulness of Whitehead's conceptuality for the appropriation of the truth of nonbiblical religious traditions is specific to Mahayana Buddhism or that Whitehead can help us in a similar way as we approach other religious traditions as well. This, too, is a difficult question. I am confident that Whiteheadian conceptuality proves fruitful in relation to some other religious traditions. I would like to think that the potential fruitfulness is universal, at least in principle, but this is not obvious.

One function of the Center for Process Studies, of which I am founder and director, is to test such fruitfulness. The Center has cosponsored conferences not only on Mahayana Buddhism but also on Chinese philosophy and on Vedanta. It is my belief that they show that Whitehead's philosophy can indeed perform a similar role in relation to dominant Chinese modes of thought to that which it can play in relation to Mahayana Buddhism.

Before approaching the most difficult question, that is, Whitehead's relevance to the appropriation of the truth of Vedanta, a word should be said about what is not being claimed in relation to Mahayana Buddhism or Neo-Confucianism. I am not claiming that the views of all Buddhist or Neo-Confucian thinkers are compatible with that of Whitehead. Obviously they are not. There are flat contradictions among Buddhists and among Neo-Confucianists, and some of the assertions of some of these thinkers flatly contradict Whitehead as well. But in relation to these bodies of literature Whiteheadians can find at their center and in what are widely considered their classic and normative formulations positions that are intelligible from our point of view.

In the case of Vedanta this is far less clear. Sankara is widely viewed as the central figure in this tradition, and although there is much in Sankara that is intelligible and acceptable from a Whiteheadian point of view, his extreme conclusions finally are not. At points at which Sankara was consciously opposing and rejecting Buddhist teaching, the Whiteheadian must sometimes side with the Buddhists.

Before acknowledging defeat in the fundamental project, the project itself must be stated more carefully. Whitehead's ideal for his philosophy was to formulate a conceptuality through which every type of human experience could be understood. I have claimed that although he himself did not understand what the distinctive experience of Mahayana Buddhists is, his conceptuality turns out to be appropriate, with suitable expansions, for dealing with it. Whitehead also believed that great thinkers are largely correct in their fundamental insights and positive affirmations, so that an adequate conceptuality will appropriate these as well. But he did not suppose that any past or present systematization of insights is free from overstatements, oversights, and distortions. He did not suppose that one could accept everything asserted by Descartes, Spinoza, Hume, and Kant, although he recognized and learned from insights in each of them.

If the features of Sankara's system which are not susceptible to appropriation from the side of Whitehead are the adequate and necessary expression of the Vedantist mystical experience, then Whitehead has failed in his goal in a serious way. This would mean that there is an important mode of human experience which no modification and supplementation of his conceptuality will allow him to interpret. If, however, the experience as such does not require these formulations, if the formulations are due to arguments which may be shown not to be beyond criticism, and if the experience can be better explained in a different way, then it is particular philosophical arguments and not a religious tradition which the Whiteheadian must reject.

It is profoundly encouraging to the Whiteheadian that one of the great Hindu mystics and thinkers of the twentieth century, Sri Aurobindo, has criticized Sankara along the same lines that a Whiteheadian wishes to follow. Aurobindo has gone on to provide accounts of a variety of levels of Hindu mystical experience and to offer a comprehensive vision of reality closely related to his own mystical experiences. There are surprisingly detailed correspondences of this vision with Whitehead's cosmology, although there are obvious differences as well. If Aurobindo offers an appropriate account of the foundational religious experience of Hinduism, then, as Ernest Simmons has shown, Whitehead's conceptuality offers a bridge to understanding this rich world as well.[2]

Although it is my present and continuing opinion that Whitehead's conceptuality can function as a bridge to the appropriation of the truth of Vendantist religious traditions, I acknowledge this to be the most doubtful case. Hindu thought has tended to substantialize in much the same way as Greek thought. It can, to be sure, be maintained that the Vedas and Brahmanas do so less, just as the Hebrew scriptures are much less prone to substantialization than Greek philosophy. Yet it is more problematic for a Christian to assert that the Hindu tendency to substantialization is a distortion of the deepest meaning of the Vedas than to assert that the similar tendency manifest in the West is a distortion of the Bible.

If we turn from these highly philosophical traditions to what is sometimes called the primal vision, the indigenous religions of Africa or of the American Indians, for example, the claim to fruitfulness is largely untested. Nevertheless, there are aspects of Whitehead's understanding of the relation of human beings to the remainder of nature which are highly promising. Also Whitehead's thought allows for modes of interconnectedness among human beings which seem to be experientially realized among those who live by the primal vision. Christians have much to learn from them, and Whitehead's thought should prove fruitful for the learning.

My conviction is that the Christianity which would emerge from these several appropriations of aspects of truth which other traditions have developed would be a different Christianity from what the West now knows. I do not, however, believe it would be less Christian. On the contrary, my argument is that in faithfulness to Christ we are to expose ourselves to these multiple transformations.

It is equally clear that the conceptuality which we employ in order to gain access to these new dimensions of truth will be modified and enriched in the process. Whether the resultant philosophy will be recognizably Whiteheadian remains to be seen. Whitehead certainly would not have cared. The process of testing against dimensions of experience with which he was not familiar is true to his intention. The resultant transformation of conceptuality is what he would have anticipated. If the new philosophy which emerges is useful over a still wider range of experience, then in the service of Christian faith philosophical thought will have been advanced.

NOTES

1. John B. Cobb, Jr., *A Christian Natural Theology* (Philadelphia: Westminster Press, 1965), p. 282.

2. Ernest Lee Simmons, Jr., "Process Pluralism and Integral Nondualism: A Comparative Study of the Nature of the Divine in the Thought of Alfred North Whitehead and Sri Aurobindo Ghose" (Ph.D. dissertation, Claremont Graduate School, 1981).

Index